No matter what i[...]
always is: How to do it[...]

The mind has ma[...]
more than you have ever dreamed of—and humanity has barely begun the wonderful evolutionary journey that will let us tap into them all at will. We grow in our abilities as we do things.

There are many wonderful things you can do. As you do them, you learn more about the innate qualities of mind and spirit, and as you exercise these inner abilities, they will grow in strength—*as will your vision of your mental and spiritual potential.*

In learning to *Meet and Work with Spirit Guides*, or See and Read the Aura, or making a Love Charm, or using a Magic Mirror, or many other strange and wonderful things, you are extending— just a little bit—the tremendous gift that lies within, the Life Force itself.

We are born that we may grow, and not to use this gift—not to grow in your perception and understanding of it—is to turn away from the gifts of Life, of Love, of Beauty, of Happiness that are the very reason for Creation.

Learning how to do these things is to open psychic windows to New Worlds of Mind & Spirit. Actually doing these things is to enter into New Worlds. Each of these things that we do is a step forward in accepting responsibility for the worlds that you can shape and influence.

Simple, easy to follow, yet so very rewarding. Following these step-by-step instructions can start you upon high adventure. Gain control over the world around you, and step into *New Worlds of Mind & Spirit.*

About the Author

Ted Andrews is a full-time author, student and teacher in the metaphysical and spiritual fields. He conducts seminars, symposiums, workshops and lectures throughout the country on many facets of ancient mysticism. Ted works with past-life analysis, auric interpretations, numerology, the tarot and the qabala as methods of developing and enhancing inner potential. He is a clairvoyant and a certified Spiritualist medium.

Ted is also active in the healing field. He is certified in basic hypnosis and acupressure and is involved in the study and use of herbs. He is a contributing author to various metaphysical magazines with articles published on such subjects as "Occult Christianity," "Working With Our Angelic Brethren" and "Metaphysical Mirrors in Our Lives."

To Write the Author

We cannot guarantee that every letter written to the author can be answered, but all will be forwarded. Both the author and the publisher appreciate hearing from readers, learning of your enjoyment and benefit from this book. Llewellyn also publishes a bi-monthly news magazine with news and reviews of practical, esoteric studies and articles helpful to the student, and some readers' questions and comments to the author may be answered through this magazine's columns if permission to do so is included in the original letter. The author sometimes participates in seminars and workshops, and dates and places are announced in *The Llewellyn New Times*. To write to the author, or to ask a question, write to:

Ted Andrews
c/o The Llewellyn New Times
P.O. Box 64383-008, St. Paul, MN 55164-0383, U.S.A.
Please enclose a self-addressed, stamped envelope for reply or $1.00 to cover costs. Outside the U.S. include two I.R.C.s or U.S. $1.00.

How to Meet & Work with Spirit Guides

Ted Andrews

1992
Llewellyn Publications
St. Paul, MN 55164-0383, U.S.A.

FIRST EDITION, 1992
Second Printing, 1992

Cover painting by Charmian
Illustrations by Christopher Wells

Library of Congress Cataloging-in Publication Data
Andrews, Ted, 1952-
    How to meet & work with spirit guides/
                     by Ted Andrews—1st ed
    p.   cm.—(Llewellyn's practical guide to personal
                              power)
    Includes bibliographical references
    ISBN 0-87542-008-7 (soft) : $3.95
    1. Spirits 2. Spiritualism 3. Channeling (Spiritualism)
I. Title   II. Title: How to meet and work with spirit guides
III. Series.
BF 1261.2.A55   1992
133.9'1--cc20   92-5767
                                         CIP

Llewellyn Publications
A Division of Llewellyn Worldwide, Ltd.

Commune with Angels . . .
Play with Nature Spirits

Wherever humans are, there are spirit beings. Many people fear contact or even the possibility of contact with an invisible realm of life. Maybe it is because humans already have so much difficulty with the visible that they do not wish to complicate things further with the invisible. At a time of increasing knowledge and psychic experiences, it is important to widen our perceptions of the spirit realm and its role within our physical lives. *How to Meet and Work with Spirit Guides* examines the realities and myths of the spirit world.

We can all benefit from contact with the spirit realm, and we often do without ever realizing it. Spirit beings serve many functions and take many forms of expression within our life. They inspire creativity, help open us to abundance, stimulate insight and knowledge, protect us and serve as our companions.

This book provides safe and easy methods to meet and work with those we call our spirit guides. It will show you how to identify them and it will eliminate fears about them. It will help you to expand your perceptive capabilities and show you how to avoid problems when opening to this realm of life.

If you wish to commune with angels, play with the nature spirits, discover your power animal totem or simply recognize the loving touch of those who have passed on from physical life, then this is the book for you.

Other Books by Ted Andrews

Simplified Magic

Imagick

The Sacred Power in Your Name

How to See and Read the Aura

How to Uncover Your Past Lives

*Dream Alchemy: Shaping Our Dreams to Transform
        Our Lives*

The Magical Name

*Sacred Sounds: Transformation Through Music &
        Words*

Forthcoming

How to Heal with Color

Magical Dance

The Healer's Manual

Enchantment of the Fairy Realm

Other books in
Llewellyn's How To Series

*How to Make an Easy Charm to Attract Love
        Into Your Life*
                Tara Buckland

How to Dream Your Lucky Lotto Numbers
                Raoul Maltagliati

How to Make and Use a Magic Mirror
                Donald Tyson

Dedication

To Mom—
Whose Spirit Touches Everyone

CONTENTS

1
UNDERSTANDING THE SPIRITUAL REALM

The ancient Greeks spoke to spirits and gods through oracles. The shamanic societies of Egypt, Africa, Bali and other parts of the world had their own techniques for establishing communication between humans and nature spirits. In the Shaker society of the early 1800s, the girls would shake, dance, whirl and speak in tongues. They claimed they were in contact with angels and spirits. In Victorian times, communication with the unseen realm occurred through spiritualist mediums. Today channelers claim communication with angels, extra-terrestrials, elves, dolphins, the Higher Self and Universal Mind among others.

The reality of beings in spirit and their assistance to those in the physical has been a part of every major religion of the world. Whether it involves angels, saints, ancestral contact, nature spirits or even demons, mystical experiences involving the spiritual realm are universal.

Because of modern distortions by the entertainment industry (movies, TV, books, etc.), misconceptions abound regarding this other dimension of life. Many believe that contact with the subtler dimensions of life requires intricate magical and mystical processes. Many assume that all spirit contact is evil, contrary to the laws of nature, and can only occur with great preparation and even greater danger. This is, of course, the stuff of fiction.

Learning to work with spirit guides in various forms is a magnificent adventure. We open ourselves to great color and wonder. We can eliminate primal fears of death and birth by connecting with those who have come and gone before. We can experience the touch of loved ones beyond the physical and learn to transform mourning into celebration.

We learn through spirit contact that we can never be truly alone, as there are dimensions of life that are open to us any time we desire. We tangibly realize the interaction of the divine within our life through such spirit mediaries, taking religion out of the realm of blind faith and placing it in that of experience. We awaken our creative imagination and intuition and our lives are filled daily with new wonders and blessings. We gain love, support and greater energy for all of

INVOCATION OF
SPIRITS OF THE DEAD*

I place this charm down beside you, subterranean gods, Kore Persephone, Ereschigal and Adonis, Hermes, the subterranean, Thoth and the strong Anubis, who hold the Keep of those in Hades, the gods of the underworld and the demons, those untimely carried off, men, women, youths and maidens, year by year, month by month, day by day, hour by hour, I conjure you, all daemons assembled here to assist this daemon.† And awaken at my command, whoever you may be, whether male or female. Betake yourself to that place and that street and that house and bring her hither and bind her.

— Greek Magical Papyrus

(The above ritual was accompanied by image magic on the grave of the person affected.)

---

* Harry E. Wedeck, *Treasury of Witchcraft*. (New York: Philosophical Library, 1961), p. 27.

†Not to be confused with the "demons" (little devils). A daemon is the spirit of a person or a god which can help determine one's fate. It could apply to the person's own genius or to a god.

our mundane tasks and responsibilities. We learn that we will never walk alone.

Through proper spirit contact we are:
- Nurtured once more by loved ones from our past.
- Encouraged by the support of angelic protection.
- Tickled by the joys and wonders of the fairy kingdoms.
- Mystified by the teachings of the ancient masters who come to life for us.
- Amazed by the spirit power of the animal world and the medicine they bring to our lives.
- Exhilarated by the diversity of life.
- Confounded by the expanse of knowledge that opens to us.
- Inspired by the spirit muses of creativity and
- Guided in all our activities.

Through it all, we are free to be who we are —in any way that we are.

Throughout this book we will examine the realities and myths of the spiritual realm. We will present you with safe and easy ways to begin to meet the wondrous beings that live with us and around us on subtler dimensions. We will show you how to take your first steps through the corridors of life beyond the physical. By doing so we will awaken new realizations, eliminate fears and empower your life.

Humans have a tendency toward smugness. We like to believe that we are the highest and the only form of intelligent life. In a universe as vast as that in which we live, such an attitude is arrogant. Just as there are many forces in the universe that we still do not understand, there are also dimensions and beings we do not understand—or even recognize.

Because we do not understand, there is often a hesitancy to explore or touch the possibilities. If given the correct information, and if approached with openness, we will see that the physical world is but a tiny fraction of all the worlds which exist.

There are those who fear contact with any being outside of the physical. Usually the ones who are so vehement about it also fear contact with other humans outside of their race, sex, religion, etc. Just as we can set limits and decide who we allow within our physical relationships, we can also select our spiritual relationships.

Yes, there are negative and ignorant energies in the spirit realm. There are also negative and ignorant energies in the physical realm. This should not prevent us from establishing relationships that can benefit us. We do not hide in our homes because we have heard there are bad people in the world. We decide who we allow in our lives—physical or spiritual. We control it.

This control begins with the proper use of discrimination regarding the relationship with spirit beings. Apply reason to the relationship and any communication from it. In cases of contact with those from the physical who have passed over, keep in mind that dying does not make a person instantly wise and spiritual. If a person was ignorant in life, there is a strong likelihood that the individual will also be ignorant in death.

Whenever we enter a new arena of study and exploration, discrimination is necessary. When it is a realm whose boundaries and influences are quite foreign and not always subject to scientific verification, it becomes even more important. Heed the words of Gautama Buddha, spoken 2600 years ago:

> *Do not believe in what you have heard; do not believe in traditions because they have been handed down for many generations; do not believe anything because it is rumored*

*and spoken of by many; do not believe merely
because the written statements of some old
sage are produced; do not believe in conjec-
tures; do not believe in that as a truth to which
you have become attached by habit; do not
believe merely on the authority of your teachers and elders. After observation and analysis,
when it agrees with reason and is conducive
to the good and benefit of one and all, then
accept it and live up to it.**

Remember, nothing within the spirit realm
can harm you as long as you maintain control and authority over your life. You should
use your relationship with the spirit realm
only to supplement and not substitute for
your life.

Spirit beings are often as interested in
establishing relationships with us as we are
with them. They can serve many functions
and take many forms. They can inspire creativity, help open us to abundance, provide
insight and information, protect or simply
serve as companions. We can all benefit from
contact with them and often do so without
ever realizing it.

This unnoticed assistance occurs throughout our life. Help we receive from our spirit

---

* Quoted in Max Muller, *Three Lectures on the Vedanta Philosophy*
(London: Longmans, Green and Co., 1984).

guides can and does occur without our knowing it. The more we become aware of their assistance and work to facilitate it, the stronger their assistance becomes. Just as there are laws that govern physical life, so too with the spiritual realms. Those who are our guides are bound by those spiritual laws. They can only assist us so much without our awareness. At that point we must consciously work to raise our energies and open our hearts to them.

The Human Essence and the Spiritual Realm

There have been numerous descriptions of the spiritual realm by many people. Mystics, clairvoyants, individuals who have had out-of-body or near-death experiences have provided diverse descriptions. It is highly probable that we each bring our own unique perception to this realm.

One of three kinds of explanations is typically given for those who experience this subtle dimension of life. The first is a dismissive explanation. The phenomenon or experience is dismissed as hallucination, fraud, error, overactive imagination, etc. The second is a scientific rationale. It is usually an attempt to demystify all aspects of the experience. For example, in cases of near death, the phenomena experienced may be explained as simply the result of *hypoxia* (lack of oxygen to the brain).

The third kind is the occult explanation. In this type, constructs are developed to explain the strange occurrence. These constructs are both philosophical and theological. In the past they have been both simple and elaborate. Although many believe most of them to be pseudo-scientific, they can provide a reasonable, philosophic explanation for that which is often intangible.

One of the most widely accepted occult constructs for the spiritual realm comes from Eastern philosophy (theosophy). In this philosophy there are seven levels or planes of existence. Each level has its own life forms and energies. Different kinds of beings operate at different levels. On the next page is a chart of some of the highest beings operating at these levels. We have access to these higher beings. The techniques in this book will assist you to learn to access and attune to beings such as these.

To understand how contact with the spirit realm works, we must understand some of the subtle constructs of the human essence involved in this theory. When we get ready

THE KINGDOMS OF THE DIVINE

*The seven planes of existence and
the great light beings operating from them.
This is just one occult construct.*

The Planes of Existence	Subtle Beings Working Through the Planes
Divine	God/Goddess, The Logos
Monadic	The Great Planetary Spirits
Atmic	Devic Lords, Masters
Buddhic/Intuitive	Avatars, Adepts
Mental	Archangels
Astral	Great Devas/Angels
Etheric/Physical	Nature Spirits and Elementals

These planes are by no means confined only to these beings. Further descriptions of these beings, along with other beings of the spiritual realm, will be given in this book. For further information on the seven planes, consult the theosophical literature which is widely available.

to incarnate into physical life our spiritual essence builds subtle bands of energy around itself. These subtle bodies are molded and aligned with the developing fetus throughout pregnancy.

These subtle bodies enable our spiritual essence to integrate harmoniously with the fetus. They serve as a bridge by which we can extend our consciousness from the physical to those more subtle and spiritual realms of life. In this way these subtle realms remain integral to us throughout our physical life. All we have to do is learn to extend our consciousness to them in a balanced, safe manner.

The subtle bodies comprise part of our auric field. The human aura is the energy field that surrounds the physical body in all directions. It is three-dimensional. There are a variety of energy fields penetrating, surrounding, emanating from and affecting the physical body. When we learn to harmonize all of the subtle energies and attune to them we open ourselves to those beings that live and operate in the spiritual realms around us. The stronger and more vibrant our auric field is, the easier it is for us to attune to all of the subtle influences in our life—including our spiritual guides. The weaker and more unbalanced our energy field is, the more likely we are to draw negative influences from the spirit realm.

Types of Spirit Guides

The kinds of spirit guides that we may encounter are as diverse as the kinds of humans we may encounter. When we begin to connect with the more subtle dimensions we may encounter both non-human and human spirit beings.

The non-human guides include those lines of life that are evolving side-by-side with humanity but are not part of its life stream. This includes—but is not limited to—angels, devas,* nature spirits and totem animals. These will be explored in greater detail later within the pages of this book, as they all have a very real and subtle influence upon all of humanity.

The human kind of guide can be living or dead (as defined by physical life). In the living category can we may encounter ordinary individuals who are out of their bodies. This often occurs at night while asleep. There can also be encounters with individuals

---

* Devas and angels are often linked together and considered part of the same evolutionary energy. Both are radiant beings. If there is a difference other than a semantic one it is that devas work more with the forces of nature.

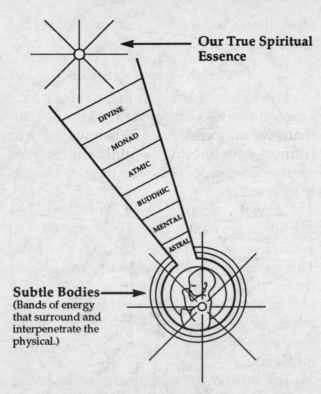

Our True Spiritual Essence

DIVINE
MONAD
ATMIC
BUDDHIC
MENTAL
ASTRAL

Subtle Bodies
(Bands of energy
that surround and
interpenetrate the
physical.)

The Incarnational Process

Our true essence slows its vibrational intensity through stages so as to be able to integrate with the physical vehicle without burning it up. These stages are the subtle bodies, bands of energies that it molds around itself so as to more fully integrate with the developing vehicle.

The consciousness does connect with the physical from the moment of conception. The connection builds, however, with increasing intensity throughout the pregnancy.

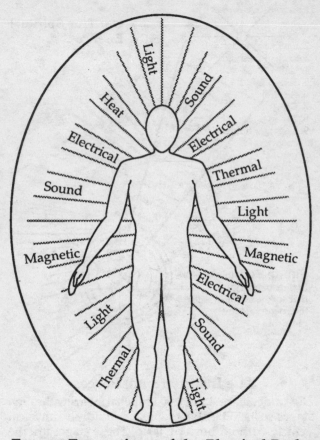

Energy Emanations of the Physical Body

There are a variety of energy fields that surround and emanate from the physical body. These include, but are not limited to, light, electrical, heat and thermal, sound, magnetic and electromagnetic. These are scientifically measurable and they help to show that the human body is an energy system.

The aura is weakened by:

1. Poor diet
2. Lack of exercise
3. Lack of fresh air
4. Lack of rest
5. Stress
6. Alcohol
7. Drugs
8. Tobacco
9. Negative habits
10. Improper psychic activity

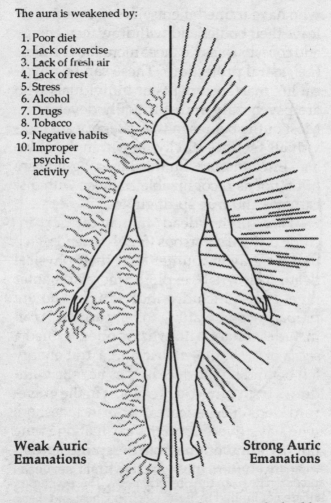

Weak Auric Emanations

Strong Auric Emanations

The stronger and more vibrant the aura is, the healthier you are and the less likely you are to be influenced and impinged upon by outside forces.

who have trained themselves to consciously leave their bodies and withdraw their energy and consciousness to those more subtle realms (i.e., astral projection). These can be physical life masters, adepts or individuals who are psychically and spiritually developing. Most of the beings in this category are individuals who are still living within the physical. Encounters with this kind of guide are often not as recognizable as those with discarnates and true spirit guides.

Those of the "dead" human category include ordinary persons (family, friends, etc.) that we may encounter after their physical death. This will be explored more in chapter nine. It also includes individuals who are preparing and waiting to reincarnate. It can include contact with what is often termed a *shade* or *shell*, the etheric and astral energy left behind by the deceased as he/she withdraws from physical life (ghost in the graveyard kinds of experiences). It can include those who have lived upon the earth at one time but are now working from the spiritual realm to grow. Often these individuals serve as guides, teachers, healers, etc. to individuals within the physical realm. It is from this category that a great many of our spirit guides originate.

Modern spiritualism has worked to categorize and identify the various tasks these guides may perform. Some of the more common categories are:

The Master Teachers—

Master teachers are usually self-realized, illumined beings. They were masters upon the earth, and thus work as masters from the spiritual realm. Examples of master teachers are John the Beloved, Abraham, El Morya, Kuthumi, Kwan Yin, White Eagle, etc. Spiritualists believe we usually only have one master teacher, but we can have more than one at certain times, depending upon our purpose in this lifetime. Master teachers oversee the growth and spiritual development of a great many people. They do not limit themselves to just one individual.

Physical Doctor—

This is a spiritual guide who works with our health and our well-being. Anyone who works to develop any form of healing will have a physical doctor. It usually is someone who was involved in healing when he or she walked the earth.

Teacher Doctor—

This spirit guide works to assist us in our spiritual growth and studies. This being assists us in understanding philosophy and is involved in all studies we undertake in any area of our life.

Chemist—

In the Spiritualist tradition the chemist is a spirit guide who works with the chemistry of our body. He assists in altering and transmuting the chemistry of our body so that we can more easily attune to the spiritual realm and more effectively handle the higher and more intense vibrations from it.

Protectors—

These guides often take the shape of large beings, strong in manner and character. It is not unusual to find protectors that are Indian or Viking in appearance. As we will see in chapter five, they can also take the form of strong animals—panthers, elephants and even dragons. These are the guides to call upon when greater strength and energy is required.

Message Bearers—

These individuals serve us in amplifying

intuitive perceptions. Individuals who develop clairaudience—the ability to hear their spirit guides—will pass messages on from them to others. These are guides that serve to assist in finding information. Many psychics and mediums use their message bearers as the source for the information they provide to others.

Door and Gate Keepers—

In some ways these guides are like the protectors. They work to keep negative entities away while the individual opens the doors and gates to the inner realms. They guard the doors so that only those guides appropriate to the situation can enter. For those who develop mediumistic trance, they help guide and guard the physical body while the consciousness is withdrawn. They allow only appropriate spirits to use the physical vehicle during the trance session.

There are, of course, many other kinds of guides. There are joy guides who work to bring light and joy into our lives. They are around whenever there is laughter. There are guides who work strictly with healing. There are lifetime guides, beings who oversee us throughout our entire life. (This will

The Symbol of Your Spirit Guide

Many spirit guides will reveal themselves through symbols, images or even specific colors. They do not always initially show themselves as they truly are. The symbol provides clues as to their function within your life. Meditation, study and reflection upon the symbol will often play upon your own energy field, raising its level so that you can more easily attune to this guide.

be discussed more in regard to guardian angels in chapter six.) There are spiritual guides who may work with us for specific purposes only. We may have a guide for only a single day or for developing a single attribute. We have family guides, totem guides, and even mythological guides.

We have what is commonly called an *inner band* and an *outer band* of guides. The inner band are those spirit guides that work most closely with us on a day-to-day basis. The outer band comes into play when we begin to work more consciously on our development. It is usually when this occurs that we meet our master teachers and become more conscious of the influence of the spirit realm.

Remember that, like us, those in spirit are energy. We will attract that energy which is most like us. Your spirit guides will be beings with individual personalities and can only be classified according to the depth, duration and type of relationship they hold with you.

Your spirit guides will make themselves known in a variety of ways. The techniques in this book are designed to increase your awareness of them and help you identify them more effectively. Some guides will use symbols. With others you will feel touches on different parts of your body. Others may be more auditory. This can range from a simple buzzing or ringing to hearing actual whispers and voices. Some will present themselves through colors or fragrances. Some may appear as creatures. Others may simply show themselves as they once were in the physical. Most spirit guides are also distinctly male or female.

Most will give names, but some will not. Names are not as important as the information that comes through the spirit guide.

Ask your guides for names anyway, as it always helps to personalize the relationship. Trust the first name you get, even if it does not seem to fit. Many guides will give you a name that you can remember and relate to. It is not unusual for the name given not to be the true name of the guide.

Guides, in whatever manner they appear, use an appearance that will be comfortable for you. It will provide clues as to their function within your life. With practice, you will be able to distinguish between your guides.

Eliminating Fears and Avoiding Problems

Here is a checklist to help you remember what to do when contacting the spirit realm so you will not have any difficulties:

1. Nothing in the spiritual realm can ever hurt you as long as you approach it with common sense and discrimination.

2. You control all aspects of work with your guides. If any display a quality or temperament that you do not like, dismiss them strongly. You do not have to tolerate ignorant behavior in your physical life and you do not have to tolerate it in your spiritual life either.

3. Although we have a number of guides assisting us, they are not watching and observing everything we do 24 hours a day. They are not voyeurs. They have other tasks to perform for their own growth. Frankly, most would be bored stiff hanging around us all the time.

4. Although many cases of possession have been reported, I have never personally encountered it. This does not mean it can't occur. When it does, there is usually something in the physical which has occurred to make it possible. Much of what the public knows about possession comes from movies and is completely false. As long as you lead a balanced, healthy life, you will never have

to worry about such a thing, even while working with your spirit guides. Additionally, the entertainment industry has fostered a belief that children are more susceptible to possession. This also is not true. Children have an extremely protective energy and a strong light about them. Yes, they often are more perceptive of the spirit realm and many "imaginary" friends are not all that imaginary. With all this, though, unless something has torn or ruptured their basic energy field (such as in the case of abuse) possession of children is nearly impossible.

5. You do not have to learn to be unconscious or in trance in order to meet and work with your spirit guides. In fact, it is best to be a fully conscious channel. It is more difficult to develop but in the long run it is safer and healthier. (This will be explored in greater detail in chapter four.) You will be learning techniques in this book to develop a more conscious recognition of your spirit guides and a fully conscious union with those supersensible realms.

6. Spirit guides will play almost any role you request. Do not become overdependent upon them and do not use them to assuage

your own loneliness or to parade around to others for the benefit of your own ego. It is amazing how much name dropping goes on in metaphysical and spiritual circles concerning spirit guides. Remember that names are unimportant. The name might have been chosen simply because it would be easier to relate to. As long as the relationship is productive and beneficial, what difference does it make if no one has ever heard of your particular guide?

7. Test the spirits. Do not follow their promptings blindly. Those who are your true guides will expect this testing and be patient with you in it. Your doubts and worries are not going to offend them and push them away. In any relationship trust is built slowly.

Chapter 10 provides ways for true discernment, testing and discrimination in working with your spirit guides.

8. Working with spirit guides is just that —work. It is a relationship involving you and them. They are not there to do everything for you, nor will they. They are not an excuse for inappropriate activity or even for inactivity. There are still people who expect their guides to do everything, or at least use

them as an excuse for their own inactivity. In the Bible we are told, "The Lord helps those who help themselves." We can adapt that phrase when describing our spirit guides: "Spirit guides help those who help themselves." Ultimately, the responsibility and the consequences of your actions (or inaction) is yours and yours alone.

9. The laws of spirit are as immutable as those in the natural world. Not learning proper techniques, rushing the opening, allowing the ego to manifest is similar to handling high voltage with no insulation or before the wires are fully grounded. It will ultimately short circuit you. There are no tricks. There are no short cuts. It does not even matter how "developed" you were in previous lives. You still must reawaken and redevelop your higher senses.

10. Contact with those of true higher soul energies is a blessing which you will feel. It will strengthen your will and enlighten your mind so that you exert yourself to reach your own goals. You will, as a result, find yourself to be more healing and compassionate in the lives of those you touch. It is not a highly esoteric process that only a

few can use and experience. If you wish to commune with the angels, simply take time to learn about them and speak to them. If you wish to talk with your guides, take time in your prayers and meditations to acknowledge them. Initiate the contact. Exactly how to do this is what this book will teach you!

2

PERCEIVING THE UNSEEN

If our spirit guides can assist us in every endeavor, why can't we perceive them? Why aren't they more noticeable? Why do we have to go to a psychic or medium to meet them? Why will they reveal themselves to a psychic or medium but not to us personally? How can some people see them when others can't?

These questions often arise when people begin to explore the unseen realms of life. The answers are as varied as the individuals who ask them. Some may have shut the doors to those subtle realms. Others may not recognize contact with this realm for what it is. This often happens with children. Their not-so-imaginary friends are usually treated by adults as if they are just the product of uncontrolled childhood fancy—often they are not. This causes the child to close down that perceptive ability.

Individuals often are unprepared to perceive spirit beings. In the Western world, because of the fundamental religious background that permeates most aspects of our society, spirit beings are often treated as angels or demons, saints or devils. People who experience guides are often treated as being evil or unbalanced.

Our society is also very rationalistic. Anything that is not immediately verified is either ignored, scoffed at or assumed to be the product of imagination. It is fortunate that the mysteries of the human mind are revealing greater powers of perception than previously accepted. This includes the perception of other realms and dimensions of life.

Another reason people don't readily experience the spirit realm is that our guides are not always with us. They do not follow us around every minute of the day. We need to learn to establish specific times and means of communication and perception. This entails the conscious development of the psychic abilities of the mind for greater contact with those spirit realms. The degree of perception will vary according to individual efforts and the amount of persistence.

Many times there is great spirit contact, but we don't recognize it for what it is. Spirit can come to us through any of our sensory organs. We may physically see them as actual beings, colors, images, animals, creatures or even symbols. They may appear as a shadow passing by or as a subtle, indistinct form. They can be seen physically or intuitively. This will vary according to the development level of your psychic ability.

We may hear spirit guides as well. This also can be internal, as well as external. Often those who are beginning to hear spirit (clair-audience) will hear soft buzzings, whispers, ringings, pops and cracks that cannot be explained through physical problems or the house settling, etc. Eventually, the sounds become distinct voices.*

It is not unusual for individuals who are developing clairaudience to awaken at night thinking they heard someone in the room or in the home. Once the adrenaline slows and they are sure no one has intruded, they need to become aware that they have sim-ply begun to perceive audible sounds. This occurs most frequently when the individual

---

* Schizophrenic personalities, wherein individuals are hearing voices continually, can be brought on by trauma, personal chem-istry and a wide variety of other possibilities. It still is not fully understood. One theory is that this kind of schizophrenia indicates a hole in the aura or energy field of the individual which allows out-side energies (and entities) to enter and play upon the individual.

is in that state between sleeping and waking. This kind of hypnogogic state is one conducive to hearing the subtle voices of spirit.

Many individuals experience the spirit realm through the sense of smell. There have been many cases of individuals who will smell the particular perfume of a deceased relative or catch a fragrance that is either associated with a guide or a family member who has passed. It can be an excellent form of personal identification and verification. When my grandfather comes to me in spirit I can identify him by a strong tobacco smell. That smell was a part of him and his room in the house in which I grew up. When I catch that unique smell I know he is around.

Some experience the spirit realm through the sense of touch. It is not unusual for a person to be out in an open field and begin to wipe at spider webs across the face. The only problem is that in an open field spider webs are not at that height. What the individual is experiencing is the touch of nature spirits.

When we come into contact with our guides they may touch us with their energy. We might feel a tingle on the arm. We may feel the a warmth or a coolness encircle us. Our head may feel like a fly is walking across it. We may feel the urge to scratch an area of the body repeatedly. With practice you can learn to identify different guides by where they touch you. You can even direct them to touch you in a specific place and manner so that you will always be able to identify the guide. We will discuss this further later in this book.

Altering Consciousness and Expanding Perceptions

Work with our spirit guides is a creative process. It involves learning to tap into the subconscious mind in a consciously controlled manner. The subconscious mind is the source of our subtle perceptions. It registers everything we encounter—physical and spiritual. A creative person is one who can process this information and these perceptions in new ways.

Accessing the subconscious is the key to more direct spirit contact. There are many ways to do this, including working with bio-feedback, dreams, hypnosis, meditation and any artistic or creative activity. Of these, meditation is one of the most effective means of awakening our perceptive abilities.

When we close our eyes and withdraw our senses from the world around us, we enter another realm of life entirely. It is more fleeting and fluid than our physical world, but it is just as real. It is a world where we can dream, ponder the future, unveil mysteries around us and discover spirit guides.

Meditation is not a difficult process. Seeing is the real problem. In learning to shift the manner in which we perceive the world we use an altered state of consciousness. We have all experienced altered states. Dreaming is an altered state. Reading often "takes people out of themselves." Jogging, needlework, long drives and listening to music are all activities which produce shifts in consciousness. Through meditation we learn to shift our consciousness in a controlled manner.

Creative imagination, or imaginative cognition, is the key to opening the doors to true spiritual awareness, energies and beings. Energy from the more ethereal realms must take the form of images for us to recognize them and work with them. The imagination should not be confused with unreality. Through it we create a new awareness of realities in form, color, sound, etc. that surround us.

Inside each of our skulls is a double brain with two ways of knowing. The different characteristics of the two hemispheres have an important role in our being able to use an altered state of consciousness for spirit contact.

Each hemisphere gathers in the same information, but they handle it differently. Often the dominant left side has a tendency to take over and inhibit the other half, especially for those of us in the Western world. This left hemisphere analyzes, counts, marks time, plans and views logically and follows step-by-step procedures. It verbalizes, makes statements and draws conclusions based on logic. It is always sequential and linear in its approach to life.

On the other hand, we do have a second way of knowing and perceiving. This is called right-brain activity. Through it we may see things that seem imaginary—existing only in the mind's eye—or recall things that may be real. We see how things exist in space and how the parts go together to make a whole. Through it we understand symbols and metaphors, dream, create new combinations of ideas and perceive the subtle energies of life. Through the right hemisphere we tap our intuition through the subconscious mind and we have leaps of insight.

One of its greatest capacities is imaging. It can conjure up an image from the subconscious mind and then look at it. These images can reflect information from the past, pre-

Left Hemisphere	Right Hemisphere
Verbal Skills, Logic, Math, Science, Language, Etc.	Music, Intuition, Imaging, Fantasy, Art, Etc.

We use altered states of consciousness to open perception to the spirit realm. It is easier to do so through the right hemisphere and those more perceptive levels of the subconscious mind. In these levels of the subconscious are the subtle perceptions of which we are usually not conscious.

sent or future. They can also reflect contact with spirit guides and entities.

There are two basic forms of meditation and of perception of the spirit realm. All others are simply variations of them. The first is a passive method. Here images and perceptions are allowed to rise to the mind as they will, forming themselves around a specific mantra, idea, symbol, etc. The second is an active method. This means you take a symbol, image, idea, etc. and mull it over to the exclusion of all other thoughts. The idea is to extract everything that you can from the idea or symbol.

All images, symbols and ideas are connected to an archetypal energy within the universe. When we meditate and focus upon it, it triggers a release of that archetypal energy into play within our life. The subconscious mind mediates this energy. On a meditative level, contact with the archetypal energy stimulates visions, impressions, feelings and intuitive insights. It also draws to you those spirit guides that are linked to that particular idea, image, etc. Their presence becomes increasingly recognizable within our outer, conscious life.

If we meditate upon ideas and images of vibrant health, the archetypal energies of health are released into our life. This in turn draws those spirit guides which can assist us in healing. If we meditate upon joy, we align ourselves with the archetypal force of joy and draw to us spirit guides which help manifest joy.

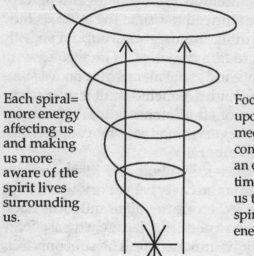

Each spiral=
more energy
affecting us
and making
us more
aware of the
spirit lives
surrounding
us.

Focusing
upon specific
meditative
content for
an extended
time opens
us to deeper
spirals of
energy.

Archetypal Energy

Image, Symbol or Idea
of Meditative Focus

As the archetypal energy is released into our life
through our meditations, the energy stimulates the
perceptive faculties. We become increasingly aware
of the subtle spirit energies surrounding us. They make
themselves known through color, symbols, fragrances,
touches, impressions and actual appearances. As we
continue meditating, the play of archetypal energy
increases in its intensity. We open to deeper spirals
of energy which leads to true clairvoyance and a
fully conscious union with the supersensible realms.

Meditation is a training of the perceptive faculties of the mind. When we fix our mind upon an idea or image with regularity, we grow more like that idea or image. This is the creative aspect of all meditation. We become that upon which we reflect. As we meditate more persistently, the fact that creative energy permeates all aspects of our life is recognizable on all levels.

It is *not* important to meditate on a wide variety of images, symbols or ideas initially. Nor is it important to make contact with a wide variety of spirit guides at the outset. Rather, it is important to concentrate on one thing and bring it to life within your soul. This will open up a conscious vision of the spiritual background of the physical world. As we learn to connect with and work with one guide fully, the others that are around us will make themselves known.

It requires only ten minutes a day of proper meditation to bring more energy and spirit perception into manifestation. Once begun, it should not be broken off out of a loss of interest or inconvenience. If persisted with for a year it will lead to true clairvoyance and a fully conscious awareness of the supersensible realms.

Spirit perception can be spontaneous or intentional. During spirit guide meditations, we use the image-forming ability of the right hemisphere of the brain to gain deeper access to the subconscious. It is here that the subtle, spontaneous contact we encounter throughout our life with spirit is registered. The exercises throughout the rest of this book are designed to assist you in developing an intentional and directed contact.

Preliminary Preparations

Enhanced psychic ability and spirit perception can be developed and used by anyone. Its development does not require higher morality any more than does the development of greater physical strength. Nor does having enhanced psychic ability and spirit perception imply that you have a high moral character or spiritual development any more than having great strength reflects it.

The psychic senses exist within us all. For most of us, however, it lies dormant. We either ignore it or refuse to develop it. Although it is a skill that is learned—just as we all can learn to read— for some it is easier to develop. There are things that we all can do, though, to help us in developing this ability:

Diet—

Some foods are considered high vibrational foods. They raise the energy levels of the human body and thus assist us in perceiving the higher vibrations of the spirit realm more easily. Fish, white meat, vegetables, pineapples, papaya, lemons, oranges, etc. are high vibrational foods.

It takes more energy to eat and digest than anything else we do. If our energy is taken up with digestion it will be less perceptive of the subtle energies surrounding us. Red meat is a lower vibrational food. It slows the metabolism and thus inhibits spirit perception. It can take anywhere from 6 to 36 hours to fully digest beef.

It is also good not to eat within one hour of a scheduled time for spirit contact or meditation. It is good to wait at least six hours if you are eating heavily.

Increase your water intake. Most people do not drink enough water as it is. When we begin to work with the high energy levels of spirit we need to increase the water. It is a conductor of energy, and it allows the attunement to occur without our becoming short circuited by its higher intensity.

Reducing salt intake is also beneficial to spirit contact. Much of our development of spirit contact is like the development of an electrical system. Just as salt can corrode an electrical line, it also inhibits the electrical impulses through the body. This makes our impressions of the spirit realm less sensitive and less exact.

Fasting occasionally is also beneficial to increasing awareness of spirit. It cleanses impurities from our system that can inhibit our perceptive abilities. The human body is a sensory organ for things physical and spiritual. The healthier the body is, the healthier and clearer our spirit contact.

Bathing—

A salt water bath eliminates toxins from the system that can hinder perceptive abilities. Use one cup of sea salt and add a cup of vinegar (to prevent drying) to your bath water. Simply soak for about 30 minutes prior to your meditation. It cleanses the etheric energy of the body and enhances perception of spirit.

Acupressure—

Acupressure is a healing technique; it is sometimes called finger acupuncture. It involves finger massage or pressure upon the traditional Chinese acupuncture points. It is a means of providing neuro-stimulation of trigger points in the body. These trigger points are found along specific nerve and energy pathways in the body. Most of its application has been for the ease of pain and the restoration of health and balance.

There are certain acupressure points that are effective in stimulating the intuitive faculties of the mind. The first points are effective in shifting energy from the cerebral cortex (the gray matter most are familiar with) to the medulla (at the back and stem of the brain). The cerebrum is that area that controls most of our conscious activities. The medulla is the center for our autonomic nervous system. It regulates the internal functions of the heart, breathing, etc. It is also the link to our intuitive sensibilities.

Along the urinary bladder meridian or energy pathway in the body is point *Yuzhen*. It is sometimes referred to as BL-9 or UB-9. Technically, these points are found on the lateral sides of the superior border of the *protuberantia occipitalis externa*. Refer to the diagram on the following page.

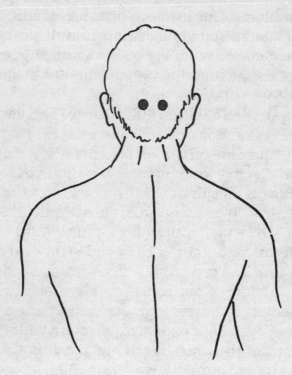

The Yuzhen Points

Massaging these points simultaneously for about 30 seconds is effective in helping to create a shift from the conscious brain activity of the cerebral cortex to that of the subconscious and intuitive brain activities of the medulla. The massage should be gentle and steady.

Gently massaging or applying pressure simultaneously to these points helps induce an altered state of consciousness. It slows the metabolism of the body and helps trigger a shift from the conscious mind to the subconscious.

Two important energy pathways for balancing the conscious mind so that intuitive perception is enhanced are the conception and governing meridians. The governing meridian runs up the spine, over the top of the head and down to the roof of the mouth. The conception meridian runs up the front of the body to a point at the tip of the tongue.

Midway between the anus and the genitals in the perineum is a point called *Hui Yin*. When stimulated in the proper manner it links the conception meridian with the governing meridian and stimulates the third eye and the intuitive faculties. Contraction of the perineum muscle (or massage of this specific point) while placing the tip of the tongue against the roof of the mouth just behind the front teeth, creates a linked circuit of energy between these two meridians.

Linking these two meridians in this manner helps stabilize the metabolism as it stimulates the intuitive faculties. This facilitates inner and outer vision of the more ethereal

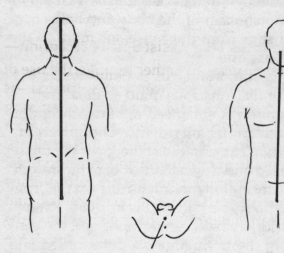

Governing   Hui Yin Point   Conception
Meridian   Meridian

An Energy Circuit

Contracting the muscle of the perineum 10 to 12 times will stimulate the *Hui Yin* point and the conception meridian. If the tongue is placed at the roof of the mouth just behind the front teeth during the contractions, the governing meridian is also stimulated simultaneously. This creates a balanced circuit of energy which activates the third eye, enhancing intuitive perception and vision of spirit guides. Rather than contract the muscles of the perineum, you may simply massage the *Hui Yin* point.

realms of life. If this exercise is being done properly, during the contraction you will feel a slight pressure in the area between the eyes.

Fragrances That Assist Spirit Perception—

Fragrance—whether through the use of herbal scents, oils, incense or potpourri—is one of the most effective means of altering consciousness and facilitating spirit contact in meditation. Fragrances alter the vibrational rate of the environment and the individual according to their unique properties. They can be very drawing to spirit guides, and they can enhance our inner perception of the guides' activities around us.

Apple Blossom

This fragrance is beneficial for connecting with the nature spirits. It is especially effective for those wishing to work with guides that may work with us through mythic images. It is a fragrance that is drawing to the unicorn.

Carnation

Carnation is a fragrance that can provide protection against spirit beings, especially the discarnate. It was worn during Elizabethan times to prevent encounters with ghosts.

Camomile

This fragrance is drawing to those devic orders associated with Egypt and Arabia. It can help you attune to the nature kingdom. Using it with the meditations in the chapter on nature spirits is beneficial. It balances the aura so that spirit perception is facilitated.

Frankincense

This fragrance is cleansing to the aura and to the environment. Its high vibration prevents intrusion by unwanted or lower level spirits. It is protective and cleansing and it enhances greater perception.

Gardenia

This fragrance is extremely drawing to the nature spirits. It stimulates telepathy, communication with the spirit realm on many levels. It can be used in rituals to draw good spirits.

Lavender

This is an herb which eases stress and facilitates altered states of consciousness. In the past, it has been carried and worn by individuals to see ghosts and spirits and to stimulate greater awareness of their presence. It stimulates higher vision, and it can be used to connect with various devic orders.

Lemon

Lemon is a fragrance that is drawing to good spirits. It was often used by old time mediums during seances to attract high vibrations and the higher spirit guides. It also assists in discrimination when working with the spirit kingdoms.

Lilac

Lilac is one of the most beneficial fragrances for connecting with the spirit realm. It helps stimulate physical vision of the subtle realms and it draws good spirits to the individual. It is very drawing to certain orders of fairies and its leaves can be used to cleanse haunted houses. It stimulates higher forms of clairvoyance.

Rose

This fragrance draws the spirit guides of love and joy to us. It can be used in spirit meditation to open connections with guides that can assist in divination and increasing psychic ability.

Rosemary

This herb, and its fragrance, is sacred to the elf kingdom. It is still used in England at Christmas as a token to elves and other good spirits for their assistance throughout the year. It is very protective in its energy and guards the individual against negative entities. When used as an oil in a bath it increases the body's sensitivity to the spirit kingdom.

Violet

Violet is the flower of the fairy queen. It is drawing to all nature spirits and it can be used to awaken greater telepathy and communication with them. Anointing the forehead with a drop prior to meditation is effective for activating greater awareness of them.

Wisteria

This fragrance has been used by occultists, metaphysicians and healers to attract good spirits and specific guides for their individual situations. It can bring you closer to those guides who will serve as creative sources of inspiration and those who will assist in developing healing energy.

A further study of herbs and fragrances will reveal much about their ability to be used to attract our spirit guides. They are not only excellent sources of therapeutic aids, but they are also effective for spiritual upliftment and heightened awareness.

Development Tools for Focusing Perception—

There are many tools that we can use to develop our psychic sensitivities. Working with them brings us into a more intuitive connection with those of the spirit realm. Such tools include but are not limited to pendulums, numerology, astrology, tarot, runes, etc. They can be used to confirm our messages from spirit as well as hone our perceptions of them. Many of the psychic development tools have spirit guides that will work with them. As you learn to use these tools, you will be drawn into contact with those guides who are assisting you in their use.

Recording Your Experiences—

It is very beneficial to record your contacts and your experiences. It serves to build a stronger foundation between those levels of the mind that perceive our spirit guides and that of our conscious mind activity. It provides a good check as to whether the spirit meditation and contact was productive or just mere fancy.

Recording the development and experiences helps you to see the quality of the communication. It provides a record for verification. And most importantly, it grounds the connection and will facilitate future spirit contact.

Recording will eventually enable you to determine if the spirit advice works. If it does, good. If it doesn't, you may have misunderstood or you may have a spirit who is not a true guide. Pay attention to what is recorded. Periodically go back and check it. Did the spirit information apply? Did this spirit contact get you into trouble? Did it help you in any way? Are you more positive and happier from the contact, or are you overstimulated? Is there simply an increasing loss of a sense of reality?

Apply common sense and record all impressions. Remember that this is a new realm for you and what applies in the physical does not always apply in the spiritual. Discrimination and verification is even more necessary. Those who are your true guides will not mind the testing. And we cannot test if we do not record accurately what has been received.

3

BEGINNING APPROACHES TO THE SPIRIT REALM

Attitude is crucial to connecting with our spirit guides in a balanced, grounded manner. If we are serious and approach it with a common sense attitude, we will succeed. Fear can block, hinder or distort the connection. If we use spirit guide contact for commercialization or to demonstrate the ego, we are more likely to encounter problems.

Contact with non-physical states has a tendency to draw our consciousness away from a physical life focus. This is why it is important to stay centered and grounded in all work with spirit guides. Our focus should be in the physical. We use contact with spirit guides to enhance physical life, not to escape from it.

In any approach to the spirit realm, we must learn to withdraw our focus from the outer and turn it to the inner. We must then learn to turn it from the inner to the outer. To do this with spirit guides can throw our energies off balance.

Here are some techniques and guides to working with the inner while maintaining balance:

1. Begin with the physical body. Proper diet, exercise, fresh air and rest is essential to balance. Work on meditation and relaxation. The more relaxed we are, the easier it is to connect with our spirit guides.

2. Work with progressive relaxation. Practice sending warm, soothing feelings to each and every part of the body. Alternately tense and relax each major muscle. This alleviates stress and it facilitates a more balanced spirit contact.

3. Learn to perform rhythmic breathing. Try inhaling for a count of four, holding for a count of four and then exhaling for a count of four. Breathe in relaxation and breathe out tensions.

4. Perform visualizations to raise your vibrations and to facilitate spirit contact. Keep your focus on the spiritual. See yourself as a

light. Now visualize a dial that runs from one to ten. As you turn up the dial your entire energy field increases, becoming brighter and stronger, illuminating all of the subtle dimensions around you and enabling you to see the spirit realm. At the end, turn the dial back down as if turning the lights off behind you. It serves to close the doors and reground you.

5. After your spirit guide meditation or contact, eat or drink something. This will kick in the digestive system and the physical metabolism, drawing the consciousness fully back into physical awareness. Do not eat heavily. Crackers or something light is all you'll need.

Many psychics and mediums use a heavy meal as a means of grounding themselves after they have done some spirit work. This can be unhealthy, and it is not unusual to find many mediums and psychics with weight and health problems.

Taking a walk or doing some light stretching exercises for about ten minutes can help re-center and ground you. Recording your experience and impressions in a journal is also a way of grounding the experience. Do something physical.

Remember, *you* set the intention of the relationship with your spirit guides. You do this through visualization, prayer, affirmation, invocation, etc. Create an inner sanctuary with imagery. One method for this is described in the last exercise in this chapter. In this inner sanctum of the mind, see a path from which someone approaches. Imagine yourself going up into higher realms from this inner sanctuary. Imagine a golden light coming to you, a light that will unfold like a flower and reveal a spirit guide. Create a doorway through which you can meet your spirit guide. Use the image-making ability of the mind to manifest an awareness of your spirit guides.

Learn to sense the vibrations around you while within this inner sanctuary. The exercises at the end of this chapter will assist you in this. Sometimes it will come as a chill from out of nowhere. The hair may stand up on your arm or neck, or it may unfold slowly —an increasing awareness that you are not alone.

Learn to identify the source. Ask mental questions about what you are feeling or experiencing. Male or female? Name? Race? Trust your first impressions—the pictures, images, symbols and thoughts that come to mind immediately after the questions. Remember, spirit guides can make themselves known in a variety of ways. How do the impressions you receive make you feel? Do you feel energized? Relaxed? Warm?

After your meditations and spirit experiences, record them. This will help you to catalogue and identify your guides. It will also assist you in verifying your impressions. Remember that different work often brings different spirit guides, and each guide may present himself or herself differently.

If you feel bombarded with impressions, mentally command them to back off or slow down so that you can register and begin to develop your relationships one at a time. It is important that you come to know the quality and character of each entity. You are the one who controls it all!

Exercises

You can use these exercises to prepare for contact with your spirit guides:

Attuning the Aura for Spirit Contact—

The stronger and more vibrant our auric field is, the more sensitive it will become to the subtle energies we encounter in our day to day activities. The following exercise is from an ancient form of mysticism known as the Qabala. It is called the Middle Pillar Exercise.* It should be used by anyone wishing to open higher faculties of perception.

This exercise employs sound in the form of ancient Hebrew God-names, visualization and breathing to fill the aura with balanced energy. It is stabilizing and cleansing, and it helps in keeping you grounded. It also will facilitate vision of your spirit guides. It can be used before and after spirit guide meditations and contact.

1. Begin in a seated position. Close your eyes and relax. Visualize a crystalline ball of light descending from the heavens which comes to rest at the crown of the head. Softly, syllable-by-syllable, intone the God-name EHEIEH (Eh-Huh-Yeh). Feel the crown of the head come alive with energy as you do this. Repeat five to ten times.

2. Now visualize a shaft of light descending from this sphere to form a second sphere in the area of the brow. Intone the God-name

---

* For more information on the Qabalah or the Middle Pillar exercise, consult the author's book, *Simplified Magic—A Beginner's Guide to the New Age Qabala* (St. Paul: Llewellyn Publications,1989.)

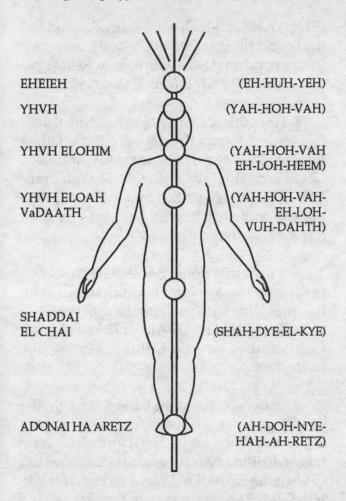

EHEIEH (EH-HUH-YEH)

YHVH (YAH-HOH-VAH)

YHVH ELOHIM (YAH-HOH-VAH
EH-LOH-HEEM)

YHVH ELOAH (YAH-HOH-VAH-
VaDAATH EH-LOH-
VUH-DAHTH)

SHADDAI
EL CHAI (SHAH-DYE-EL-KYE)

ADONAI HA ARETZ (AH-DOH-NYE-
HAH-AH-RETZ)

The Middle Pillar

JEHOVAH (Yah-Hoh-Vah) softly. See and feel the sound fill that area of the body. Feel your inner eye coming alive with energy. Repeat this five to ten times while feeling the energy grow.

3. From this second sphere the shaft of light descends to form a third sphere of crystalline light in the area of the throat. Vibrate the God-name JEHOVAH ELOHIM (Yah-Hoh-Vah-Eh-Loh-Heem). See and feel this sphere of light come to life with brilliant vibrancy. Repeat five to ten times.

4. From this sphere the shaft descends to the heart area to form a fourth ball of light. It comes alive with each intoning of the God-name JEHOVAH ALOAH va DAATH (Yah-Hoh-Vah-El-Loh-Vuh-Dahth). Repeat five to ten times.

5. Pause and visualize the shaft of light descending from the heart to form a fifth sphere in the area of the groin. See it form with crystalline brilliancy with each intoning of the God-name SHADDAI EL CHAI (Shah-Dye-Ehl-Kye). Repeat five to ten times.

6. Now pause and visualize the shaft of light descending from this fifth sphere down to

the feet. Here a sixth crystalline ball of light forms and the shaft continues on through it into the heart of the earth, grounding and balancing you. As you tone the God-name ADONAI HA ARETZ (Ah-Doh-Nye-Hah-Ah-Retz), see this sixth sphere of light come to life.

> *You have now formed the Middle Pillar of balance which extends from the heavens, through you, to the heart of the earth. You have activated the inner centers of light which will strengthen and protect you, along with awakening your spirit vision.*

Bring your attention back to the crown of your head and begin rhythmic breathing. As you exhale slowly to a count of four, see and feel energy pour down the left side of your body. Inhale for a count of four and draw the energy up the right side. Repeat this four to five times.

Now the energy shifts. As you exhale, see and feel the energy stream down the front of the body for a count of four. As you inhale, allow it to rise up the back. Repeat this four to five times.

Bring your attention to your feet. Feel the energy gathering there. Now as you inhale, the rainbow colored light is drawn up through the pillar to the crown of your head. As you exhale the rainbow light is sprayed out the top of your head to fill your entire aura with strength and energy. Repeat this four to five times. Now pause and allow yourself to bask in this brilliant energy field.

Once you have performed this exercise several times, you will become aware of its affect upon you. Then, as you allow yourself to bask in this renewed energy at the end of the exercise, open your senses to those of the spirit realm.

Keeping your eyes closed, extend your senses outward. Pay attention to any new or different sensations, ones not normally felt when you do this exercise. Do you have a feeling of a presence? Are any particular colors standing out in your mind's eye? Do you feel a tingling, a pressure or a change of temperature? Are there any fragrances? Do you sense anything different?

Don't force it. The new impressions will come softly and naturally as your own energy field becomes stronger and more sensitive through the Middle Pillar exercise.

Ask mental questions. Is there a guide close to me? Are you male or female? Will you identify yourself with a touch? Pause and use your senses. If you feel something, ask that it be repeated. This will help confirm that it is not just your own mind.

If there is no touch, ask for a color, a symbol, a fragrance, a face. Ask for some form of identification. If you do not get it initially, do not be discouraged. As you continue, your efforts will be rewarded.

When you do get a response, continue the mental questioning. Name? Purpose? Visualize yourself having a conversation with this being. If a symbol is experienced, see this symbol before you and imagine a voice coming from it to answer your questions. If it is a color, imagine a large glowing ball of this color before you from which comes the voice. If it is just a touch, imagine the space in front of you where you think your guide is standing. Remember that the imagination serves to helps us access the subconscious which is attuned to all subtle energies and entities around us.

The Mystic Marriage—

This exercise activates and aligns the upper four chakra centers of the body. It increases the flow of energy to them and it enables greater use of our intuitive and higher-self capabilities. This in turn facilitates recognition of our spirit guides. Take your time with this exercise. Pay attention to the sequence. This is what helps induce the altered state or "alpha brain wave" state which enables us to see spirits more easily.

1. Bring your attention, your consciousness, to the area between the eyes. This is the area referred to in metaphysics as the Third Eye. It is the seat of our intuitive perceptions. It is the center that facilitates physical vision of the subtle realms of life.

2. Envision this area as glowing in brilliant crystalline light. As you inhale, see and feel this area warm and brighten with this light. Hold for a count of ten. Exhale slowly, and then repeat three times.

3. Now as you inhale, draw the light backward from the brow area through the head to a point near the crown of the head. This is the area of the crown chakra. This chakra awakens higher-self consciousness and union with the spirit realm.

4. As you visualize this ball of light moving backwards, also imagine a bridge of light—

a *rainbow bridge*—being formed between the brow and the crown chakra. See and feel it as warm and shimmering with energy.

5. Hold the focus of the light in the crown area for a count of ten and then exhale slowly. Repeat three times. Feel the warmth and energy filing your entire head.

6. Now bring your consciousness, in the form of that brilliant light, down to the throat area. See it as a rainbow bridge extending from the crown center to the throat. Here is another major chakra or energy center. This center is aligned with our creative will and the ability for clairaudience—hearing spirit.

7. As you inhale, feel this center come alive with crystalline brilliance. Hold the breath for a count of ten, as with the other two centers, and then exhale slowly. Repeat at least three times. Imagine and feel the energy and light intensify with each breath.

8. Now draw the consciousness and energy down from the throat to the area of the heart. See this as yet another extension of the rainbow bridge. Feel the area of the heart warm and begin to radiate with crystalline energy.

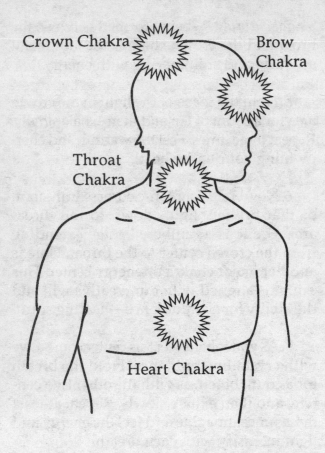

Crown Chakra

Brow Chakra

Throat Chakra

Heart Chakra

The Mystic Marriage

This exercise activates and aligns the upper four energy centers. This activation stimulates our higher faculties of perception. We thus are able to sense and perceive the spirit realm more easily.

9. Inhale, holding for a count of ten. As you hold your breath, feel the energy intensify, and as you exhale see and feel the link that has been formed with the other three energy centers. Exhale slowly and repeat at least three times. You have now activated the higher centers of perceptions.

10. You must now complete the circuit. Draw your consciousness and attention upward from the heart back to the third eye in the area of the brow, completing the rainbow bridge that connects all four centers. Feel it grow with new intensity and energy from having activated and aligned itself with the other three.

This exercise is a guideline. Adapt it to yourself. Remember that it is the breathing and visualization that stimulates the higher faculties associated with these centers into activity.

At this point you may extend your perceptions to the area around you, just as you did at the end of the Middle Pillar Exercise. Begin the sensing and the questioning.

As you sit relaxing at the completion of the Mystic Marriage, extend your senses outward. Pay attention to any new or different sensations. Is there a feeling of a presence? Are any particular colors, feelings, touches or tinglings, being experienced? Do you sense anything different? Pay attention to everything, no matter how slight. Remember that this exercises increases our physical and spiritual perception.

Don't force it. The new impressions will come naturally as you begin to activate and strengthen these higher centers. Remember to continue the questioning—especially if you are getting some response—even if you are not sure where it is coming from. Don't forget to record your impressions. Keep in mind that a relationship does not unfold all at once. It is built, little by little, with each day adding to its depth.

It is even more effective to use this exercise as a prelude to the following one. It will facilitate the imaging and visualization, and it will increase perception of your spirit guides in that sanctuary.

Creating the Inner Sanctuary to Meet Spirit Guides—

An effective way of increasing your awareness of your spirit guides is by creating a special sanctuary within the mind and consciousness where you can go to initiate communion with them.

Use your imagination in creating this sanctuary. It should be a place you can visualize and will feel comfortable and protected in. It can be a temple scene, a place out in nature, or a castle in the clouds. It is a place of intersection where the physical and the spiritual realms can meet. It is a point in the heart and mind where there is a thinning of the veils between the two worlds. It is a place where those in spirit can approach you on your own terms. The more you develop it in your mind, the stronger your own spirit contact will be through it.

This sanctuary will be yours. You can create it and change it as you go along. Initially, you may wish to use the following scenario, but do not lock yourself into it. It is to serve as a guideline to help you begin to develop your own inner spirit sanctuary.

1. Begin the exercise by making sure you will not be disturbed. Take the phone off the hook, etc.

2. Set the atmosphere with candles and fragrance. Choose one of the fragrances touched upon in chapter two.

3. Close your eyes and relax. Perform a progressive relaxation or some form of rhythmic breathing. The more relaxed we are, the easier it is to access the subconscious mind and stimulate it into revealing spirit contact.

4. Perform the Mystic Marriage Exercise. It is an excellent prelude to this meditation. It stimulates the imaginative faculties and awakens the intuition.

5. Now visualize the following scenario. Imagine it. Make it real with the creative power of the mind:

As you relax, draw all of your energies around you, as if someone has placed an old, comfortable quilt about your shoulders. You are relaxed and at peace. There is a sense of anticipation, for you are about to be introduced to one of your spirit guides.

Within the darkness of the mind a scene begins to form. Faintly you hear the sound of water, a soft, gentle stream that must be close by. There is the sound of birds, and you begin to feel the warmth of the sun upon you. You smell the gentle scent of spring flowers and new-mown hay. A soft breeze caresses your face.

You look about you and see that you are in a small, circular garden. The color of the flowers stands out strong against the greens of the grasses and trees. Surrounding the garden are stately oaks, their branches extended as if protecting you.

You breathe deeply of the sweet air. You are relaxed and at peace. You know this place. You have seen it before. Maybe in your dreams or maybe in a distant lifetime—it doesn't matter. You just know that it is your haven. It is a place where you can go to heal and refresh yourself. It is a place of life and peace.

You see that you are sitting upon a stone. It seems to have been carved out as if to be a chair for you within this garden. It makes you feel solid and connected to the earth.

As you look about, renewing your memories of this sanctuary, you see a path that leads down from a distant mountain to this garden. This path is lined with stones of every color and kind.

At the opposite side of the garden, you see this path continue. It leads out from the garden down to a distant valley. As you look down this path, you see your present home within that distant valley.

You understand that you are at a plateau, an intersection of time and place. It is an inner sanctuary where the real and the unreal meet. It is the place of the finite and the infinite, the physical and the spiritual. Knowing this is freeing. It relieves you of stress and worry. In this place there is only "to be."

As you sit upon your stone chair, you see up the path toward the mountain a small, golden light. It seems to draw closer and closer to you. It floats gently up the path toward your little sanctuary.

Its light is soft and gentle, yet it shines with a brilliance you have never seen. As it reaches the outer edge of your sanctuary, it stops, a large pulsating crystalline light.

You watch, waiting, but it doesn't move. It stays just outside your garden. This puzzles you at first. Then you remember. This is *your* garden. Nothing can enter without your permission. You find this thought to be very comforting.

You slowly stand and take a step forward. You nod your head, acknowledging the light and giving it permission to enter. The light draws forward and hovers just before you.

The light shimmers. Soft strands of gold stream forth from it. The light seems to unfold itself, like a flower blossoming. As each petal of this light unfolds, you see that something or someone is inside. Then you see before you a wondrous being! See it. Imagine it. Know that it is real.

As you look upon this being, pay attention to what you experience. Are there specific colors? Fragrances? Do you feel a touch or tingling on any part of your body? Is the being male or female? Even if the unfolding only reveals a symbol, that symbol can reflect a male or female energy. Trust your impressions.

Begin to carry on a conversation in your mind with this being. Ask it its name. What is its purpose? Why is it around you? How can you come to recognize it more consciously in the future?

Don't force the answers. Let them come naturally. Let this being communicate about itself to you, tell you why it is working with you and what it will help you accomplish in the future. Ask your guide how best to call upon it in the future.

Don't worry that you might be imagining it all and that it may all a product of the mind and not a reality. You would not be able to imagine it at all if there wasn't something real about it.

Now bring the conversation to a close. Ask your guide for something that you can use to verify its reality. Is there something coming up in your life that you need to be aware of? Is there something important that you need to know? Ask it for a touch, a tingle or some kind of physical sensation at a specific time over the next couple days. Make it a reasonable request, one that is easily fulfilled and confirmed.

Now thank your guide for the opportunity to meet and work with it. As the golden light folds back up around your guide, send it off with your best thoughts and love.

As it withdraws from your garden, moving back down the path, you sit back down upon your rock. You understand that in this inner sanctuary you can invite all of your guides into your awareness. This is exciting, and you are excited about the opportunity of expanding your horizons.

You breathe deeply, relaxing and reliving the conversation in your mind. As you do, the garden begins to fade. You find yourself sitting in your home, comfortable and peaceful, remembering all that you have experienced. Slowly and gently open your eyes, aware for perhaps the first time that there is life and energy on all dimensions around you.

6. At this point it is good to record your experience with your guide. Write down all that you saw, felt or learned. This will help

you in grounding your energies into the physical, and it will help you in remembering your individual guides.

Also record any new impressions you may have about this spirit guide. Sometimes insight into our spirit guide's energy comes to us when we are in the recording process. We understand more fully some of the information passed on to us during the encounter.

7. Fully center and ground yourself back into the physical. As discussed earlier, this can be accomplished by eating something or some kind of physical activity.

One of the most effective ways of recentering and grounding ourselves is through the use of the Middle Pillar exercise. It also helps us assimilate and integrate the new energy we received when we contacted the spirit realm. It helps us to become acclimated to it so that we remain balanced and grow stronger in our ability to commune with the spirit realm.

Testing and Developing Rapport

As you begin to initiate greater contact with your spirit guides it is important to do some testing to verify that the contact is not just uncontrolled fancy or wishful thinking.

This testing can be done in a way that helps develop a greater working rapport:

1. Ask for specific messages for yourself. This should be information that you can use. It should also be applicable within a reasonably short time. In this way the information can be verified and confirmed more easily, and we can establish trust more quickly. When I encounter a new spirit guide I ask for information that can be verified within a week to 10 days. This, of course, will vary according to the individual purpose and function of that guide within my life.

For example, a guide who is working with me on business and finances may be requested to provide information or a new opportunity that can be verified within a specified period of time. If it does not occur, re-evaluation is important. Maybe the time frame was not fair or maybe the guide was not legitimate. Test several times. Don't draw conclusions from one time only. Not everything in the physical can be determined, controlled or directed by those in spirit—nor should it be.

2. Ask for messages for friends. See if they bear out. This will also help you develop trust.

3. Ask for favors from your guides. Make sure they are reasonable requests. Asking to have the guide help you win the lottery is not a reasonable request. They are to assist us in changing our own lives. They are not to do it for us.

A good favor to ask of your guides is to find you parking places. This works well. Visualize the area you wish to park, close your eyes and ask your guides to reserve you a space either exactly there or right near there. I rarely have to search for parking spaces. Usually the only times I do is when I forget to ask for that favor.

Ask for their assistance during times of transition. Remember, though, that they are willing to help but cannot do it all for you. This can be anything from helping to smooth out problems to eliminating possibilities of hassles.

Ask for your guides to send you dreams that will help you work with them more fully. Some guides will work specifically through dreams and can help you in learning to control your dreams.

Ask your guides to place things in your path for you. This can be opportunities or certain kinds of people. Remember they can help us to open doors, but we have to walk through them.

5. Take an occasional walk with your guides. Arrange, through meditation, a time in which you are going to take a walk, and ask your guide to come along. Carry on mental conversations with your guide during this walk. Use the walk as a form of inspirational meditation.

4

MEDIUMS AND CHANNELS

Mediumship and channeling is more than just a modern day phenomenon. Communication with spirits, angels and even the deceased has been around as long as humanity. In the ancient world the Oracles of Delphi are probably the most famous. On the slopes of Mount Parnasus was a long deep chasm in the rocks. A vapor issued from the chasm. A temple to Apollo, the god of prophecy, was erected here. A priestess called the *Pythia* would sit upon a tripod over the seat of the fumes. After some time the fumes would induce a trance-like condition and she would speak in phrases that were considered divinely inspired. Questions were answered and prophecies uttered from this oracle one day per month.

Even in the Western world where fundamentalist Christians are quick to condemn such activities as evil, scriptural references are found in support of it. The Biblical Witch of Endor communed with the spirit realm for King Saul and even Jesus conversed with Moses and Elijah before the apostles Peter, James and John (Matthew 17: 1-8). These are merely two of many such references.

In the modern world we have seen a growth and rebirth in this communication process. In 1843 a near-illiterate by the name of Andrew Jackson Davis drew attention to the spirit realm through his ability to see into it and use knowledge from it to cure diseases. He became known as the Poughkeepsie Seer.

The Fox sisters (Katie and Margaret) are considered the first spiritualist mediums in the United States. In 1848 they heard rappings alleged to be communications from spiritual beings. Using information from these rappings, the girls discovered that a former occupant of their house had been murdered. Although psychic researchers speculate that they drew poltergeist activity because of their age, their activities created a wave of interest in spiritualism.

The birth of modern spiritualism in the mid-1800s would lead to the influence of such famous figures such as Arthur Ford after the turn of the century. Arthur Ford was a Philadelphia medium who, through his seances, allegedly made contact with the dead son of Bishop James A. Pike. He helped establish the Spiritual Frontiers Fellowship which at one time boasted membership of leaders from every major faith.

One of the most famous and most influential mediums of modern times was Edgar Cayce. A deeply religious man from Hopkinsville, Kentucky, as a child he spoke with an angel and even saw visions of his dead grandfather. Through trance, he treated over 30,000 patients. He provided accurate readings on health, personal and social matters and even gave long-range predictions of geological changes and world events. As familiarity with Edgar Cayce spread, so did the possibility of spirit communication.

The mediums and oracles of the past are now the channelers of the present. These include J. Z. Knight and her communication with a 35,000 year old discarnate entity called Ramtha. It also includes such figures as Jane Roberts who channeled Seth and Jach Pursel and his communication with the being known as Lazaris. These are but a few.

So what is mediumship and channeling? To the modern spiritualist, a medium is defined as one "whose organism is sensitive to the vibrations of the spirit world and through whose instrumentality, intelligences in that world are able to convey messages and produce phenomena."* While channeling also encompasses this definition it has come to imply much more, for mediumship has come to be associated with communication with discarnate individuals and the proving of the survival of the personality after death.

Channeling also involves a sensitivity to the spirit realm, but it has become a catch-all term for most forms and phenomena of the psychic and creative realms of life. A person who has creative inspiration says they channeled it from some source (often indefinable). An actor channels his/her character. When Hal Holbrook portrays Mark Twain, he could be considered a channeler by many people, although to many he is simply a gifted interpreter. This demonstrates the catch-all aspect the term "channel" has acquired. Hopefully, by the end of this chapter, you will have a truer idea of channeling and trance.

One who is intuitive is channeling perceptions from the higher self or soul. One who discovers a new form of healing, a new thought, a new perception, a solution to a problem or a new invention can be considered channel-

---

* Anon., *The Spiritualist Manual*. (Cassadega: Nationalist Spiritualist Association of Churches, 1980), p. 40.

ing. The channeling can be an actual spirit guide contact or it can be an image of a spirit guide contact from your own intuition and Higher Self. The difficulty arises in defining the source of the channeled material and proving its legitimacy.

Most literature teaches us that there are levels and dimensions of reality beyond the physical. If this is true, it should also be possible to connect with them. Mediumship and channeling are forms of extra-dimensional communication. Whether this is done through telepathy (although some believe that telepathy only applies to two embodied persons), intuition, trance or any of a variety of methods for altering consciousness is irrelevant. It is the message, the communication which will determine the worth of the channeling. It is the accuracy of the information which provides the true evidence of the phenomena.

Many believe that the messages only appeal to those who are discontent and uncreative in their own lives. Some of these communications are nothing more than empty platitudes for such individuals. Some channelers and mediums use the stuff of fiction and wishful thinking to draw attention to themselves. They are taking material advantage of this "modern spiritual band wagon."

Many who were lucky to get any attention now use pseudo-accents and proclaim elaborate, unprovable sources for their channeling material—all with great success.

Many channelers incorrectly believe they are in true contact with a particular being or master. For example, a person who channels Jesus may not truly be channeling Jesus. This may only be what he or she is capable of understanding that energy to be. It is as close as he or she can get to defining it. This isn't wrong in and of itself, but it is misleading. It indicates the need for a great deal of spiritual knowledge and maturity before ever placing yourself in a position of channeling and counseling for others.

Does that mean we should disregard all aspects of spirit contact and channeling? No. There are those who demonstrate strong evidence of the more ethereal realms by their communications. This includes contact with the deceased, communication with masters and teachers, contact with the angelic and the nature realm and even connections with extra-terrestrial life. The difficulty lies in determining the true from the false, the real from the illusionary.

This is a very powerful and magical time to be living. It is a time of greater stress and energy. It is a time of greater knowledge and awareness of the mystical aspects of life. Because of this, greater discrimination and care in the development process is even more important.

With the greater accessibility of knowledge there has been a tremendous influx of teachers in the metaphysical and psychic fields, many of whom do not have the appropriate background and schooling. Many have failed to learn how to independently test what they themselves were taught. The process of "becoming" is time consuming, and many people do not wish to put forth the time and energy necessary for true knowledge and discernment. Many do not wish to take on that part of the responsibility.

There are quick ways of rending the veil to higher perceptions and levels of consciousness, along with opening to direct contact with other entities. However, if the wires cannot carry the load the current will become distorted, burnt out or misinterpreted. Channeling is very popular today, and there are individuals teaching how to do forms of trance channeling in weekend or week-long seminars. This can be dangerous, especially if the energy of the individual has not been properly cleaned, cleared, strengthened and prepared.

Often those with just a little knowledge feel they are constantly in control when in reality they are not. Even if the techniques have been learned in previous lives (which many channelers credit for their facility at the process), it still requires proper training to reanimate them in a beneficial manner. Regardless of the degree of initiation a soul may have gone through in the past—even if in the past the soul had been a master—it would still have to reconquer the lower and re-educate the higher self and expand it by renewed effort. Even the Master Jesus had to go through this process.

For true channeling to occur in the most beneficial manner, there must be individual preparation and purification. This includes a greater, in-depth knowledge of the spiritual sciences. Surface and superficial techniques and learning will not maintain you for long. Attempting to do so will result in a breakdown of your energy at some point—physically, emotionally, mentally or spiritually.

The key is understanding the function of our etheric body, one of the subtle bodies mentioned in chapter one. The etheric body is the densest of the non-physical bodies. It vitalizes, energizes and protects the physical vehicle. It serves to ground the consciousness into physical life. It also filters out the more subtle energies and dimensions of life so that we are not overly distracted. Our primary focus is to be in the physical. It is this band of energy which is usually first detected by someone working to see the auric field.

The etheric forms around the physical body anytime between birth and puberty, most often between the ages of four and eight. Until the etheric body forms entirely, the astral plane (one of the more subtle dimensions that integrate with the physical) plays upon us and is recognized more fully. It is not filtered out. For this reason, many of the so-called imaginary playmates of young children are not really so imaginary. They are beings and entities of that plane.

Once the etheric is formed much of the subtle plays of energy are filtered from the conscious mind, although the subconscious will still be able to perceive them. As we grow and mature we can work to reopen our conscious awareness of those subtle realms. To do so we must learn to extend the consciousness out through the etheric to the realms beyond.

Lying between the etheric and the astral is a thin band of energy sometimes referred to as the atomic shield. It is like a thin layer of atoms that filters out the stronger astral energies from physical consciousness. These are the strongest feelings and emotions that could play upon us and affect us.

When we begin active development, we must loosen this shield. We must stretch it for greater flexibility. This will enable us to extend our consciousness to the astral dimension and beyond. This stretching must be done carefully. It is comparable to the warming up before any strenuous exercise. It will help prevent injury. If we were wishing to compete in gymnastics, we would go through a very lengthy period of daily training and work to develop flexibility and strength before we ever attempted anything too intricate.

Using improper techniques of development can create problems in your energy field. All of the following can make you more susceptible to tears and holes in your etheric energy field:

- Using drugs
- Opening to trance too soon
- Lack of concentrated, prolonged effort
- Lack of knowledge

- The inability to control your energies
- Not taking care of all aspects of your health
- Lack of exercise and fresh air
- Poor diet
- Negative habits
- Continued stress, upheavals, worries and emotional/mental traumas

Once that atomic shield is injured it is difficult to stop influences from outside energies until it is corrected. This may require closing down and shutting off all occult or metaphysical activities for a prolonged period.

Many of the more famous individuals who opened to trance and the subtle realms through quick methods are just now beginning to demonstrate problems in their lives. These include physical health problems, emotional and mental imbalances, etc. Initially they may have opened to some very high, positive energies and entities. Because of the manner in which they opened (a tearing in the shield), however, over time other entities and energies were able to play upon them more actively. The individuals were not able to guard against the outside intrusions 24 hours a day although this is what was and is necessary when the energy field has been torn.

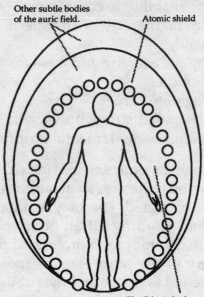

Other subtle bodies
of the auric field.

Atomic shield

The Etheric body
(Inside the Atomic Shield)

The Atomic Shield within
the Human Energy Field

The atomic shield is a thin band of energy separating the etheric and astral bodies. It grounds the consciousness to physical life while filtering out the more subtle dimensions of life. As we begin to develop, we must learn to stretch and expand that atomic shield so that we can extend our consciousness out through it without tearing it. This creates a fully conscious union with those subtle dimensions of life. Proper meditation, concentration, exercise, fresh air, spiritual knowledge, and general health all strengthen and facilitate our ability to do this successfully.

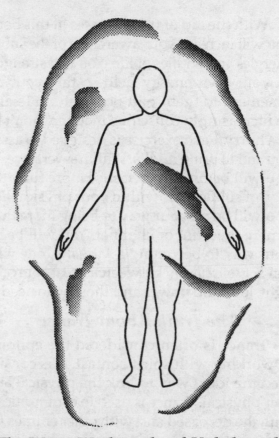

The Way a Weakened and Unbalanced Aura may Appear

An aura (energy field) that is weakened and unbalanced is more susceptible to tearing. This leaves a hole in the field which is draining to our overall energy and enables outside energies and entities to play upon us more dynamically. Such an aura may appear to look like this.

With the aid of the exercises in this book you will increase your awareness of the subtle energies and entities of life. You will strengthen your own energy field so that your attunement to them will occur in a safe and an increasingly conscious manner. Don't be in a hurry. Each exercise is designed to assist you and to bring results. Within several weeks you will begin to experience more fully the play of subtle lives within your physical life. You will be on your way to being more than a mere medium or channel. You will be on your way to becoming a *Mediator*, one who can act *consciously* between a great source of light, love and power and those who need it.

The Truth About Trance

Trance is often considered the epitome of working with spirit contact. It is considered the ideal way to link the physical and non-physical. Trance is used to communicate with the deceased and with other entities for inspiration and knowledge. It is an altered state of consciousness. Probably the most famous practitioner of such trance work was Edgar Cayce.

"A trance channel is simply a person who has developed the ability to set aside one level of consciousness and allow another level of consciousness to come through."* This, of course, could be another level of consciousness within yourself or another consciousness outside of yourself. What few realize, though, is that there are different kinds of trance and varying degrees of it. All must be prepared for and developed.

There is the occasional demonstration of spontaneous ability for trance such as in the case of Edgar Cayce. This is the exception, however, rather than the rule. Therefore we should be wary of individuals who proclaim such spontaneous ability as the result of past life preparation, as a special gift of God, as simply an unexpected mysterious occurrence of the present, as the result of a major trauma within life or even as the result of an injury. All of these indicate there is very likely a rip or hole in the aura.

There are two kinds of trance. The first is mediumistic trance. This kind of trance usually takes one of two forms of expression. In one of them, the individual's ego withdraws from the physical body, turning it over to a spirit guide or spirit being to communicate through. Memory is often limited or non-existent. In the second form the indi-

---

* Kevin Ryerson, *Spirit Communication*. (New York: Bantam Books, 1989), p. 5.

vidual becomes extremely passive and receptive as in the first form, but it doesn't withdraw entirely from the physical body. This receptive condition enables the spirit to overshadow and override the personality and ego of the individual. Both forms of mediumistic trance are passive conditions. They are *not* active powers.

The second kind can be called shamanic trance. It is the basis of the vision quest or the shamanic journey. In this form of trance the individual's ego withdraws from the physical body while leaving it protected. The soul then explores other dimensions, communicates firsthand with spirit guides and entities, and then returns with the information in full memory and consciousness. In this form there is control. It is more active.

All altered states of consciousness, including trance, are most easily developed through the use of guided imagery meditations and visualizations. These serve to build a bridge between the physical world and the more ethereal realms. They help us learn to control the mind stuff, what in yoga is termed the *citta*. By stilling and focusing the mind with images you can become more aware of the inner realms and can more easily develop a conscious interaction with them.

Most occult techniques for spirit contact are simple. They depend upon effective meditative abilities that can be developed by anyone. These techniques are based upon three fundamental abilities that must be developed: visualization, concentration and creative imagination. These lead to higher forms of inspiration and a fully conscious, intuitive perception of the spirit realm.

Visualization is the ability to create a mental picture and hold it steadily within the mind. It should be as life-like as things within the physical. A simple exercise is to visualize an orange, clearly seeing its shape, size and color. Feel the skin on it as you press your fingers into it to peel it. Notice the fragrance as the juice squirts out. Then create an image of its taste.

Concentration is the art of holding an image within your mind without the mind wavering or wandering. We should develop the ability to concentrate our focus to hold an image to the exclusion of all others. Practice closing your eyes and counting to ten slowly. Focus exclusively on each number until the next is sounded. If you find your mind wandering or have such thoughts as "Oh, this isn't so difficult," then your concentration needs work. You should be able to count slowly to

100 with little or no distraction. (If you are part of a meditation group, alternate individuals counting to 10 or 20 as a preliminary exercise at each meeting. Do not count in a regular rhythm or speed that can be anticipated. This forces greater concentration.)

The third ability is *creative imagination*. This enables the mind to create images and scenes associated with the purpose of our meditation. These created images should be in three-dimensional form. They are like a highly concentrated daydream or actual dream in which you become completely absorbed within the framework of the scenes, losing awareness of the ordinary world around you. This creative imagination, or imaginative cognition, is the key to opening the doors to spiritual energies and beings.

How do we tell if what we are experiencing is a reflection of our creative imagination or an actual spirit contact? When beginning with meditational exercises, we observe ourselves experiencing a particular situation or we imagine how it would be experienced. In a true shamanic journey or shamanic trance, we are actually within it. We feel and experience it all first hand, and it will not necessarily follow a prescribed pattern.

The soul learns to permeate ideas, images and symbols in meditation to gain entrance into the soul-spiritual realm. As we develop the ability to assume a union with our meditation symbols, we begin making transitions from the pictures to their supersensible origins. We are moving from a passive awareness to a conscious interaction when our work and exercises begin to take this form.

We open the doors through the imagination. Then we begin to explore through inspiration. This opens ourselves to direct spiritual perceptions themselves rather than perceptions of images that must be translated.

As you work with the exercises in this book, you will encounter varying degrees of trance and altered states of consciousness. A light trance state is a generally relaxed state of being. When we are relaxed we are more open to non-physical influences. The breathing should be gentle and easy, as if you are going to sleep. It is important though that consciousness be maintained. Relaxed alertness is the key. This is all that is necessary to develop contact with the spirit realm.

In deeper levels of trance the individual can become unconscious to the surroundings. In many ways this is like going to sleep, only without the snoring. (In this book we will only be dealing with methods for consciously controlled trance states.) It is always more beneficial to develop and control our faculties than to simply sit, waiting to be used as an instrument. Consciously controlled spirit contact involves taking your development in hand.

5

TECHNIQUES FOR SPIRIT MEDIATORSHIP

Rather than being a mere medium or channel, we should strive to be a *mediator*. A mediator is one who has the ability to act consciously between a great source of light, love and power and those who need it. This individual will always know with whom he/she is in contact. There will always be awareness of what the nature of the message is, whom it is for and how best to convey it so as not to inadvertently influence or intrude upon the free will of the recipient.

A mediator knows exactly the source of all messages and is capable of phrasing them in a manner to which that the individual will be able to relate. Because of strongly developed mental and intuitive capabilities the mediator will also know how the recipient will probably respond to the message. The mediator is able to test and verify information and messages because of a strong and deep education in all of the spiritual sciences and because of control over all of his/her energies. One who is serving as a mediator does not have to be perfect in all of these things but should be striving for them.

A mediator should have control over all perceptions and sensibilities on all dimensions. The true mediator should be able to turn his/her perceptiveness on and off at will. This form of positive, controlled intuition and soul impression should only be used consciously at the right time, in the proper manner and degree for the correct individual. There are great karmic responsibilities and repercussions in mediatorship.

Unfortunately, many who establish spirit contact assume that they are ready to serve as mediators for others. True mediatorship can never be fully developed if we begin working with the public or the outside world too soon. Your contact with the spirit realm will change your energy levels. These energies need to build up in order to transmute old conditions to higher perceptions. Working with the public too soon will dissipate the energy that would otherwise have been used to transmute your lower aspects into higher forms of perception.

It is important to understand that being able to contact and communicate with your spirit guides does *not* make you a mediator. It requires great training and skill, not only in the spiritual sciences but in such areas as human behavior, counseling, etc. Not everyone should be a mediator, but we all can benefit by communication with the spirit realm in the form of increased inspiration, higher teachings and healings.

There is a misconception about the psychic world and the path to higher spirituality today. Many assume that if they are not working actively in the field they cannot be making progress. They feel that if they are not demonstrating psychic ability, they are not growing. We must be careful about having a desire or need to be out front, displaying our abilities.

It is not the demonstration of psychic ability, higher intuition or type of spirit contact that unfolds our potential. It doesn't even reflect it. Our potential and the reflection of it can be seen in the meeting of our daily trials and obligations in a creative manner that propels us along our individual paths.

The purpose of contact with the spirit realm is not psychic power, but expanded perceptions. It is the development of the ability to look beyond physical limitations and learn the creative possibilities that exist within them while at the same time transcending them. It is to help us rediscover the wonder, awe and power of the divine universe and how it lives within us.

Mediatorship Exercises

The following exercises will help you to attain the desired goal of being a mediator:

Sitting for Development—

Group sittings and meditations can be wonderful ways to initiate spirit contact. It is usually best to begin your awakening to the spirit realm in a group situation. Like-minded people, coming together for a common purpose, will generate energy that is stronger and more vibrant as well as facilitate spirit contact. It also enables the individual members to become comfortable with spirit contact. Old deep fears and superstitions are less likely to intrude or distort your impressions.

It is good to have at least one member of the group who is knowledgeable and has spirit perception. This person will help to control and direct the process, preventing premature trance and unforeseen problems.

1. Plan on the sitting to occur once a week, at the same time and preferably at the same place. This lets your spirit guides know when and where to be present. Each gathering or sitting should be at least one hour. The sittings should last for a cycle of at least three months.

2. Be prepared to use any aids necessary to keep the energy strong and vibrant in the area of the sitting. This can include the use of incense, candles, music and song. Some groups will gather in a room in which a red light is used to help keep the energy strong.

3. Prior to arriving for the sitting, refrain from eating for at least an hour (preferably three hours). If the body is working on digestion, it is less likely to attune to the more subtle energies. Taking a detoxifying bath (see chapter two for details) is also of help. Determine ahead of time—and inform all members ahead of time—of the seed idea, thoughts or image that the group will focus on that night.

4. If the group is small enough, sit around a table. For larger groups, arrange the chairs in a circle. Any socializing before the actual sitting should be done in a room other than the sitting room. This prevents the energies

from being disturbed. The group should enter into the room at the same time. Stragglers are disruptive to the balanced energy and can hinder or delay spirit contact.

The sitting room should be prepared before anyone arrives by being cleaned and by having incense already lit and burning.

Once the group has been established and has started sitting together, new members should not be permitted. It takes time to establish group harmony. Once the group has sat together several times, the threads of this harmony are sown. New members can create an unraveling and delay the process.

5. Once everyone has taken his or her place (it should be the same each time), have the evening's leader make some consistent gesture to let the group know that it is time to settle in and prepare for a shift in consciousness. This may be an act as simple as the lighting of candles or the turning on of a red light.

6. Begin the sitting by joining hands and reciting a prayer, affirmation, invocation, etc. This can be performed as a group or each individual may take a turn leading it. Traditionally, some groups will sing a song or two to raise the energy.

7. At this point, perform—as a group—the Middle Pillar Exercise or the Mystic Marriage. (The Mystic Marriage can be effective at the beginning of the sitting while the Middle Pillar Exercise is an effective closing.) The designated leader for the evening should direct it. At the conclusion of the exercise, the leader can direct the group's attention to the seed thought or image for the evening. Something general, such as "joy" or a symbol, can be used. Some brief comments upon it, no more than 30 seconds or so, can also be given.

8. As the group sits meditating upon the night's purpose, general relaxation or a light trance will ensue. Pay attention to what is experienced. Do you notice any lights or twinklings in the room? These are often called *spirit lights*. Do you feel any tinglings, pressures or changes in temperature? Mentally make note of what is experienced. If it continues, do some mental questioning as described earlier.

Anyone who feels so impelled should verbalize what comes to mind concerning the evening's focus or what is being experienced. Don't worry that what is said may sound foolish. As you communicate what you are impressed with, the lines of communication will open wider.

I often hear individuals mention that they see or feel something, but do not know what it means. People must understand that if they could not understand or relate to it in some way it would not be coming to them. In such cases, have the person describe what he or she sees or feels. The verbal description alone will begin the clarification process. It is not unusual for a light to click on even before the description is completed. We must first open the lines of communication—then we can go about interpreting them.

9. Do not worry about the source of the communication at this point. With time this will clarify itself. Don't place too many expectations on the sitting or the communications. Speak what you are inspired to speak. Do not be upset if you have nothing to say. Be considerate and allow others the opportunity to share. The lines of communication open at different rates for different people, but they will open for all if they persist.

10. Before long, the guides for those in the group will begin to crystallize. Within four to six weeks each member will begin to

recognize at least one guide. As the group continues, this will expand. Some guides may only come in for an evening. Some may come into the group to pass on one particular message. Keep in mind that you may get information about your own spirit guide from someone else in the group, just as you may be impressed with information about another's guide.

11. Occasionally introduce songs to keep the energy of the group in harmony and at a higher level. At the end, offer a prayer or an expression of thanks to those guides, recognized and unrecognized, for their presence. Then as a group, perform the Middle Pillar Exercise as a formal closing to reground and balance all members of the group.

12. The group should leave the sitting room together. Having snacks available at the end is a very effective way of further ensuring grounding.

Do not enter into sittings with preconceived notions. Keep your aspirations high. Don't ask too many questions. Don't let spirit rule your reason. Define and describe fully what you are experiencing before you attempt to interpret it.

Be courteous in the message bearing. Make sure you make your own decisions, and do not try to consult with spirit on all things. Do not be concerned with periods in which nothing seems to occur. Part of the process of sitting for development involves the raising of the energy of the entire group to facilitate spirit communication.

Keep records of all your communications. Later that evening, when you are at home, fill in your spirit guide journal. This can even be done as a group as a post-sitting activity. This will help you crystallize messages and often brings further insight to the spirit communications and impressions.

With time, the group *can* bring its attention to specific problems and concerns. Begin slowly. Do not force the communication. Let it flow naturally. Persistence brings results.

Inspirational and Automatic Writing—

If you prefer not to work with a group, using inspirational or automatic writing is one of the easiest methods for development. In more distant times, there were two predominant tools to assist with this—the *Ouija board* and the *planchette.*

The Ouija board is a flat board upon which are letters, numbers and the words "yes" and "no." Although today it is often treated as more of a game, it is a tool that many have used in the past. The fingers are placed lightly upon its planchette (a pointing device which glides over the board) and a question is asked of the spirit realm. While concentrating upon it, spirit is supposed to start the planchette moving, pausing over various letters to spell out messages.

It is not a tool that I recommend for opening to spirit communication. It has an energy that draws lower entities to it. These entities can create problems. When not in use it should be covered and put away. It serves as an open door, especially to discarnates and to earthbound souls. (Refer to chapter nine.)

The true *planchette* was designed to be a tool specifically for automatic writing. The individual would place his or her hand flat upon the heart shaped device, with the pencil between the first two fingers. The person would then use an altered state that would allow a spirit entity to move the planchette about on the paper, writing out specific messages. The spirit entity superimposes its will over the normal functions of your hand to spell out a communication.

You do not need these devices to open your ability for inspirational or automatic writing:

1. Set a definite time to spend on these efforts. This is most effective when performed at the same time each day.

2. Sit comfortably with pen in hand and notebook ready. Plan on giving yourself a half hour for this on a regular basis.

3. Begin with a prayer and an intent. You may even wish to set the atmosphere with incense or fragrance and candle light. Perform a progressive relaxation. Perform the Mystic Marriage. Offer a prayer for guidance and protection, then mentally invite any of your spirit guides to enter.

4. As you relax, pay attention to what you feel. Initially remain passive and quiet. Meditate and focus upon recognizing the touch of spirit. When you are relaxed, mentally call out and invite a spirit guide to draw close. Pay attention to what you experience. Do you sense anything? A color? A sound? Any pressure or tingling? Is there any change in temperature? Write down any impression you get, no matter how slight or seemingly insignificant. (Remember that you are learning to recognize the approach of spirit, and it won't necessarily be strong in the beginning.)

5. This step is sometimes difficult for some individuals, but it is very effective for opening the lines of communication. After receiving your first impression, continue to sit with pencil in hand, resting them upon the paper. Keep your eyes closed and begin a conversation with the guide who has approached you. Don't worry that you may be imagining it all. Remember we work with the spirit realm through the imaginative faculties to build up to conscious perception.

Ask the guide questions and write the answers down on the paper as you receive them. Do not open the eyes to do this, and don't worry about whether the writing is scribbled. Keeping the eyes closed prevents outside distractions and helps you to maintain the altered state. After some time the ability to record the conversation with the eyes open will develop. Begin with such questions as:

- Would you touch me again? (You can also designate the spot you wish to be touched. This will help you distinguish this guide from others.)
- Are you male or female?
- Are you around me often?
- When am I more likely to recognize you?

- What purpose do you serve in my life?
- In what area of my life will you be more prominent?
- What is your name?
- Is there a particular color, sound or fragrance that will draw you closer?
- Can you show me, in my mind's eye, what you may look like? (Don't be discouraged if this does not occur initially. Persist and it will. When it does occur, you may wish to try and sketch it in your journal.)
- Is there anything specific I need to know at the moment?
- How can I help assist our attunement?
- Are there any other messages that you have for me?

6. Write what comes to mind. Keep writing. Don't worry that the thoughts may be disconnected. Don't worry about its grammar or structure. Initially you are just setting up the energy of receptiveness to the inspiration of spirit. Allow your thoughts to flow in response to the questions and write them down. Don't try and think about them or analyze them. Simply record them. At the end of the half-hour, you can go back and review them.

7. You are opening the lines of communication. First with your own intuitive self, and secondly—and ultimately—with your spirit guides. As you persist, you will find that your writings will begin to take on a certain distinct personality and flow.

Once the relationship and the lines of contact are established, each guide will begin the communication and end it in a distinct way. When I first began this I found that the communication with one of my spirit guides always ended with the image of a flower—nothing elaborate, just a simple flower. I drew this, just as I recorded all other impressions in the session.

8. At the end of the allotted time, stop and perform a closing. Offer a prayer of thanks to those guides who have drawn near, whether you recognized them or not. Perform the Middle Pillar Exercise to ground yourself.

When you move from inspirational to automatic writing you will find your hand beginning to make squiggles and circles. Your hand will seem to do what it wants to do. There will seem to be no feelings in the hand and it will take on a mind of its own. This may continue for several weeks before anything recognizable appears on the paper.

Persistence is the key. This has great potential. I have seen individuals who perform tremendous automatic drawing. The art work is very intricate and often faster than the eye can follow. One individual often has his eyes closed during the drawing or may be involved in talking and discussing something entirely alien to the face within the picture.

There is much to be learned about altered states of consciousness and the creative faculties we can touch within ourselves and within other realms. It is that discovering process which provides much of the adventure and wonder of learning to connect with the spirit realm, especially through inspirational and automatic writing.

Scrying with the Crystal Ball—

Crystals have recently gained tremendous popularity as a metaphysical and psychic tool for the individual. However, there has been little exploration in the use of the more ancient and traditional crystal ball. The electrical properties within the ball will stimulate inner vision (the third eye). The crystal ball is a dynamic tool for scrying in the spirit and for opening seership of the spirit realms of life. By learning to crystal gaze we can open ourselves to vision of the spirit realm, to images of the future and even those of the past.

The size of the crystal ball is not as important as your willingness to work with it. It should be several inches in diameter so that you will be able to peer into it without straining your eyes. Some individuals profess that a clear quartz crystal ball is much better for scrying than a ball that has configurations, planes and other formations within it.

I have found it makes no difference. It is simply a matter of personal choice. I am in possession of several crystal balls of differing sizes and varying clarity. The one I use most frequently is about three inches in diameter and it is milky with several unique formations.

Every seer uses the crystal ball a little differently, but each will follow certain guidelines in discovering his or her own unique approach to scrying with the crystal ball.

1. The crystal ball is usually kept in a special place—a cabinet, a room, etc. This prevents others from handling it and drawing off its energy or leaving their own energy imprints upon it.

2. A small stand or sturdy table is used with the crystal ball.

3. Keep the crystal ball clean. A mild soap solution is effective and can be used periodically. The ball should also be covered when not in use. A black silk scarf is effective for this. The silk scarf not only protects it from dust, but it also insulates the ball from outside energies.

4. The crystal ball should be charged and energized periodically. As with any crystal, setting it outside for 24–48 hours is very effective, especially if it is around the time of the full moon.

5. Each crystal gazer must bring himself or herself into harmony with the ball. Meditate with it. Simply hold it and perform rhythmic breathing is also an effective way to gain harmony with it. A traditional method involves "making passes" over the ball. The scryer imparts strength and energy into the ball by passing the right hand over and around it while the left hand is believed to impart sensitiveness into the ball. As you handle it you will begin to feel comfortable. Take several minutes a day to perform this.

If it is not a clear ball, take time to examine the various configurations and planes within it. You will find that these will change as you work with your crystal ball. Each time you scry they will take on different forms.

It is important to be patient and to concentrate when using a crystal ball. There is no good or bad time to use the ball, except according to your belief. Yes, astrological influences can heighten or lessen the effectiveness, but it is not necessary to understand these to be able to achieve results.

Take time to make sure you will not be disturbed. Perform a relaxation and even the mystic marriage. This will further heighten the crystal ball's ability to awaken your clairvoyance. Use a prayer, affirmation or other form of invitation to your spirit guides.

Have the ball before you so that you can easily gaze into it. It is better if the lights are dimmed, as the ball can pick up and reflect the light, hindering your vision. Having the ball resting upon a black cloth or background is also effective. This will prevent glare and reflection from the surroundings.

Hold within your mind the question or perhaps the desire to see your spirit guide. Using a soft gaze, look into the ball itself. This gaze is similar to those times when we stare vaguely off into space. It is not an intense focus, but a relaxed one. Pay attention to what appears. Do not be discouraged if nothing initially occurs.

The phenomena seen within the crystal ball will vary. At first, clouds are often seen. It is like the crystal is fogging over in spots. This can be a kind of milkiness or even seen as clouds drifting across the ball. This is a positive sign. It is an indication of coming clarity and vision.

Clouds, colors, images, faces and then entire scenes will eventually come to you as you work patiently and persistently with the crystal ball. Initially, the difficulty arises in interpreting what is seen. Remember that the images and vision within the ball will be in response to what you are focusing on in your mind.

If you are trying to attune to a spirit guide, the color of the clouds may provide a clue to the guide's energy, purpose and/or function in your life. The shape and movement of the cloud can also provide clues. Trust your impressions.

Some believe that clouds moving upward are positive, while those moving downward within the ball are negative. Some believe that clouds moving to the right are indications of spiritual beings, while clouds moving to the left indicate this is not a good time for scrying. This will vary from individual to individual. Some of the interpretation of what you see will be trial and error, but the more you work with it, the better you will become.

Continue this for 15 minutes. Then close down. Cover the ball and perform some closing and grounding ceremony. The Middle Pillar Exercise is beneficial. Even if nothing seems to occur, know that the gazing is increasingly affecting your clairvoyant ability. With persistence, your efforts will be rewarded.

6

MEETING OUR GUARDIAN ANGELS

We exist in a living universe. There is life and energy and an order in everything around us—whether it is visible or not.

As humans we have a tendency to walk around with blinders on. We train ourselves to recognize only that which is visible, that which is rational. Maybe it's because we have such difficulty with physical life that we don't want to be bothered by the possibility of an invisible life. Whatever the reason, we do limit our perceptions. Unfortunately, that also limits the possibilities within our rational world.

There is a line of life evolving side-by-side with human development. They have bodies of lighter substance which are often invisible to our heavier sensibilities, but they embody the creative intellect and the transmuting energy of the universe. They are the Angelic

Hierarchy, and much of the good we know in this world is the result of their work—whether it be the beauty of nature, creative inspiration or the wonders we refer to as miracles.

We do not have to be aware of their presence to receive their benefits, just as we do not have to be constantly aware of the air we breathe. Yet they are as nourishing to us and as essential to our lives as that air.

Most people consider angels the stuff of fiction, especially in this age of intellect and science, but they have been active in history in every age and every race. We can't prove to everyone's satisfaction the reality of their existence, but with increased awareness we can each begin to experience them in our own ways. One of the most profound joys in life is feeling the comforting breath of their wings upon the shoulders. It inspires joy, love and wonder at the magnificence of the universe.

Humans are smug. We like to believe that we are the highest form of life. It is true that we have a divine spark, but so do countless numbers of other life forms. Many of these life forms express that divine spark more radiantly and more consistently than we do. It's very likely that even the lowest angel is more highly evolved than the uninitiated human, especially when we consider the things humans have done to each other and the planet.

When we were children we glowed when called an angel. Intuitively we knew that it was something special. On some level we probably knew it signified being enlightened. An angel is a being capable of disseminating the divine light into all religions and all lives that are less evolved.

Angels appear in all literature and in all religions. They have been written about in story and song, and they can be found in half the books of the Christian Bible. In the Book of Psalms (Ps. 91) we read, "He hath given his angels charge over thee to keep thee in all thy ways."

There are myriads of entities in this hierarchy. They are called messengers, sons and daughters of the Divine, spirits, holy ones, devas, shining ones, nature spirits, seraphim, cherubim, thrones, dominations, virtues, powers, principalities, archangels or simply angels. Whether we experience their love through our spirit guides, through nature, through religion or even directly, it should strengthen and encourage us to know that those above us desire to lift us gently to higher realms.

The functions of angels include praising and attending to the Divine, protecting the faithful and guiding humanity. There are angels of power, healing, home, nature, art, beauty and creation. There are angels for every aspect of life, and if nothing else, it should reassure us that we do not have to do anything alone.

The archangels are the interpreters of the higher orders and they serve as mediators between humanity and the divine powers of the universe. The nature spirits and angels work for the rhythmic unfoldment of the universe through the forces and expressions of nature, whether it be assisting a blade of grass to grow or assisting the movement of the planets and stars throughout the universe.

Every child knows of guardian angels, but much about them is misunderstood. We are all under the watchfulness of a group of angels who assist us while not doing for us. As we yearn for greater spirituality and begin to work more consciously for it, we will come under the guardianship of a single angelic being. This being will serve as a teacher and initiator through the ordeals that lead to greater spiritual maturity. In the ancient Hebrew tradition, this guardian angel comes from a group known as the *Malachim*, angels of healing, light and miracles.

Our consciousness is broadened by considering the existence of beings unlike us in physical nature yet one with us in service to the Divine. It is said that with a child's first laughter, an angel is born. This could be because it is such a simple loving response to life. As we age, we lose that simplicity. We cling to the known and the visible and expect sameness, instead of realizing the infinite differences and possibilities with each passing second.

The angelic hierarchy show us how to realize what we are by their example. They execute their tasks with a creative joy, resourcefulness and color far beyond our own labors. There is no drudgery in their work for they realize that each task has its place in the scheme of evolvement and glory.

We need to do likewise. We need to raise our scope, remove our self-imposed blinders and begin to view the whole picture. The angels will assist us in this. All we need do is ask. These androgenous beings (neither male nor female, encompassing qualities of both)—from their vantage point and from their loving and willing interplay with our consciousness within the rhythms of the world —can see what we truly are. They see the true essence of our being.

The angels see the steps we need to take in the times ahead and are capable of connecting us more quickly to our divine origins. All we need do is open our hearts and extend our hands to them. Then we too can fly upon the wings of angels.

The Four Great Archangels

There are many associations for the great archangels of the universe. Many people have tried to define and delineate their individual responsibilities, but we must keep in mind that there is great overlapping. We may say that one is for healing and another for protection, but at that level within the hierarchy they each can perform any of the functions of the others. There are simply areas of greater focus and responsibility for them.

Four of the multitude of archangelic beings work intimately with the earth. These four are Raphael, Michael, Gabriel and Auriel. Associated with each of them are one of the four elements of the earth, specific colors, one of the four directions or quarters of the earth, three signs of the zodiac and a variety of energies and powers. Understanding these associations and looking at them in relation to ourselves can help us determine with which of them we are more likely to resonate.

Raphael—

- Element of air
- The eastern quarter of the earth
- The spring season
- The color blue (or blue and gold)
- The astrological signs of Gemini, Libra, and Aquarius

Raphael is the *healing* archangel. This being works to stimulate energies for life and success. Raphael awakens a sense of creativity and beauty which stimulates higher mental faculties. Raphael is the Keeper of the Holy Grail.

Michael—

- Element of fire
- The southern quarter of the earth
- The summer season
- The color red
- The astrological signs of Aries, Leo, and Sagittarius

Michael is the archangel of *protection and balance.* This being works to bring patience and protection against any psychic imbalances or dangers. Michael helps us to tear down the old and build the new.

Gabriel—

- Element of water
- The western quarter of the earth
- The autumn season
- The colors of emerald and sea green
- The astrological signs of Cancer, Scorpio, and Pisces

Gabriel is the archangel of *hope, illumination and love*. He guards the sacred places of the world and the sacred waters of life. He provides intuitive teaching and illumination of spiritual duties. This includes awakening within us a greater understanding of dreams.

Auriel—

- Element of earth
- The northern quarter of the earth
- The winter season
- The color white and all earth tones
- The astrological signs of Taurus, Virgo, and Capricorn

Auriel is the Archangel of *alchemy and vision*. This being is known as the tallest of the archangels with eyes that can see across eternity. Auriel oversees the work of all nature spirits and works to assist humanity by awakening to them and working in harmony with them. Working with Auriel will open you to the fairy kingdoms.

There are several simple methods of determining which of these four great archangels you will have the easiest access to within your life. The first is through your astrological sign. The archangel who rules your sign will be the one with whom you most resonate. The astrological sign is an energy signature, a matrix of a specific stellar pattern that will subtly influence and affect you. For example, if you were born in the sign of Cancer, you will have a greater ability to resonate with Gabriel than the others. This doesn't mean you cannot connect or relate with the others, but the one associated with your birthdate may be easier.

Another way of determining which archangel(s) you may have greater ease at connecting with is by looking at the elements within your name. The vowels are associated with the specific elements of fire, air, water, earth and ether (the source of the other four). Use the chart on the next page and determine which elements are found within your name and which archangel rules that element.

This name element and its archangel may differ from the archangel of your astrological sign. This simply means that you have a greater ease at connecting and resonating with both. If you were born in the sign of

Cancer, the archangel is Gabriel. If your *primary vowel** (the vowel most strongly pronounced) in your first name is "I" (such as in the name Timothy), you are related to the element of fire and thus the Archangel Michael. Therefore from your astrological sign and your name, you can most easily resonate and connect with the archangels Gabriel and Michael.

DETERMINING YOUR ARCHANGEL FROM YOUR NAME

Primary Vowel	Element	Archangel of that Vowel
E	Air	Raphael
I	Fire	Michael
O	Water	Gabriel
U	Earth	Auriel
A	Ether	All four archangels
Y	Fire & Water	Michael & Gabriel

Exercise to Meet One of the Four Great Archangels—

Once you have determined which of the four archangels you are most likely to res-

* For more information on this I refer you to my earlier book, *The Sacred Power in Your Name.* (St. Paul: Llewellyn Publications, 1990)

onate with, you can begin the process of opening the doors to closer contact and communication. You can use simple meditation techniques to facilitate this connection.

In the technique that follows, we will build on the previous exercises for spirit contact. First we will introduce the use of sigils (symbolic signatures for the archangels). The sigils provided on the next page are signatures based upon the Golden Dawn technique of tracing the Hebrew letters of the name on the symbol of the rose on the rose cross.* There are many other ways of forming these sigils.

When we meditate upon them they serve as call signals to those energies that they represent. In this case, they serve as call signals to the archangels.

1. Make sure you will be undisturbed.

2. Light incense or use a fragrance according to your purpose.

3. Perform rhythmic breathing and progressive relaxation. Remember that the more relaxed you are the easier it will be to attune to these beings.

---

*Israel Regardie, *The Golden Dawn*. (St. Paul: Llewellyn Publications, 1986), pp. 9–47.

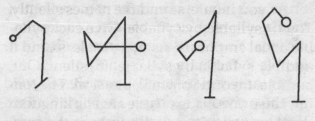

RAPHAEL	GABRIEL	MICHAEL	AURIEL
(Blue)	(Green)	(Red)	(White)

4. Perform the Mystic Marriage Exercise to activate your inner vision.

5. As part of this exercise you will call forth to the archangel you seek. This involves *toning*. Each of the archangelic names have three syllables when toned and spoken properly. This indicates the inherent energy and influence of the archangelic kingdom. Three is the number of new birth, creation and of the Holy Child Within who is born out of the union of the male and female within us.

It is good to practice the toning before the meditation, although in the meditation you may simply wish to project the sounds mentally. Toning the archangelic names is very stimulating, protective and balancing, and can be used periodically to keep the aura strong and to help maintain health.

As you inhale, sound the names silently. Tone it syllable by syllable. Give each syllable equal emphasis. As you exhale, sound it audibly syllable by syllable. In, silent. Out, audible. In, out. Spiritual, physical. The toning helps you bridge to the angelic kingdom and also serves to call the archangel closer.

RAPHAEL   =   Rah-Phah-Ehl
MICHAEL   =   Mee-Kah-Ehl
GABRIEL   =   Gah-Bree-Ehl
AURIEL   =   Ah-Ree-Ehl

6. Visualize a door forming before you. It is the color of the archangel you are working to connect with. Engraved into this door is the sigil for that archangel. As this image becomes clear, perform the following meditation:

You are standing before the door. With your hand you reach out and trace the engraved sigil. As you do, the door begins to vibrate softly. It is like a gentle hum. You take a step back, unsure of what is to come.

The door begins to open inward. As it does it spills a light that is bright and crystalline. It is the color of the door and of that associated with your archangel. It streams over you, passes through you and then softly

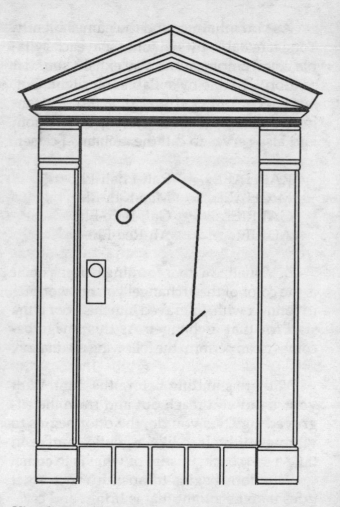

Visualize and imagine a door forming before you.
Engraved into this door is the sigil of the archangel
you are seeking to connect with. See this door in the
color appropriate to the archangel.

surrounds you. It invites you across the threshold into the realm beyond the door.

You step across the threshold and the door closes behind you. You are surrounded with color and soft sound. It is as if the colors themselves are singing to you in greeting. You see before you a sea of color—varying in shades, tones and depth. It is all based on the color associated with the archangel you seek.

In the distance is a vague cloud of brighter hues. It holds its place in this realm where everything else is shifting and blending. You understand that it must be invited, called forth.

Softly, hesitantly, you tone the name of the archangel. The distant cloud brightens. With greater confidence you again tone the archangelic name. The cloud shimmers and floats softly before you. A third time you tone the archangelic name. As you do the cloud of crystalline light shimmers, and from it steps a magnificent being of beauty and light.

The energy radiating from this great being is like wings enveloping you, filling you and lifting your heart. Never before have you felt that your heart could sing, but at this moment you know it truly can.

In your mind your hear your name sung. You never knew that it was so musical. You raise your eyes to this wondrous archangel.

Its eyes hold you fixed. They are older than time and filled with strength and unconditional love. As you look into them, images pass through your mind. Images and whole scenarios.

You see the places in your life where this great being has aided and assisted you without your knowledge. You see images of times and places you do not know. You see scenes of new life and new adventure and new joy as you learn to work with this wondrous being.

As the images fade, this archangel steps forward, embracing you. You hear a message whispered within your ear. A gentle kiss upon your head sends shivers of delight throughout your body and soul. You are filled with a feeling of exquisite joy.

Aware of a new power within you, gently you reach out with your heart and your mind, daring to touch this magnificent one. For a moment the intensity is too much to endure, but for a few brief seconds you find yourself at one with this Being of Light. You know that your life will never be the same.

The archangel steps back into that cloud and the cloud recedes softly into the distance. The door behind you opens, and with another glance back you step across the threshold to the outer world. As the door closes, you understand that it is never truly sealed. It is a door that will help you to fly upon the wings of angels.

Other Aids to Angelic Contact

Many traditions speak of the angelic contact that occurs through the signs of the zodiac and through the planetary influence. General aspects and qualities associated with each sign and each planet, as found within any general astrology book, will help you determine how these angelic beings are likely to be affecting your life.

There are angels of the sign Cancer who assist individuals with their feeling nature and angels of Aquarius who assist us in seeking ourselves. There are angels working through every sign. As each month passes and a new astrological sign comes into play, the influence of that particular group of angels working through that sign is felt more strongly by everyone. They are also more easily attuned to during that month. A good monthly meditation is to visualize that same door, engraved with the astrological symbol of the sign of the new sign of the zodiac. Then you should walk through the door and commune with the angels of that particular astrological sign.

Visualize in your angelic meditation, a door engraved with the astrological symbol of the planet and the archangelic sigil. See the door in the color associated with that planet and sigil. In the above case, the door would be visualized as green and it would have the symbol for the planet venus and the sigil for the Archangel Haniel. (These correspondences are based upon the mystical Qabala. Refer to author's previous books on this subject.)

 **Saturn (♄)**
Archangel: Tzaphkiel
Color: Black

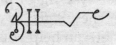 **Jupiter (♃)**
Archangel: Tzadkiel
Color: Blue

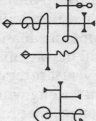 **Mars (♂)**
Archangel: Kamael
Color: Red

 Sun (☉)
Archangel: Raphael
Color: Gold

 **Venus (♀)**
Archangel: Haniel
Color: Green

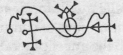 **Mercury (☿)**
Archangel: Michael
Color: Orange

 Moon (☽)
Archangel: Gabriel
Color: Violet

Sigils for the Archangels and Their Planets

There are also archangels associated with each of the major planets. Many of these, especially those of the seven major planets, have been given sigils. These sigils, as well as the glyph for the planet, can help you in attuning and connecting with the archangel of the planet. This can be used to help you understand planetary influences within your life.

Simply adapt the previous meditation to that of the planet. Make all the preliminary preparations, but this time visualize the astrological glyph for the planet, along with the sigil for the planet's archangel. (For further information on the color associations used in the diagrams on the previous two pages, refer to the author's book *Simplified Magic: A Beginner's Guide to the New Age Qabala*. St. Paul: Llewellyn Publications, 1989.)

Work with the angelic realm should always be creative and joyful. As you learn to work with the previous angelic meditation, adapt it to fit your self. Find new ways of communing and connecting with the angelic hierarchy:

1. Study literature which refers to them. Become as familiar with them as possible.

2. Use prayer and meditation to contact them and to be drawn into contact with oth-

ers who may be working to see and understand them.

3. Spend time in nature.

4. Become involved in anything creative or artistic. You don't have to be good at it; simply enjoy it. This brings greater contact with the angelic hierarchy.

5. Use music to open to them, for they almost always come with a song.

The angels are drawn to anyone who is working toward self-mastery. If you persevere in remembering them and in remaining open to them through expanded awareness, you will feel the touch of their wings within your life.

7

WORKING WITH
THE NATURE SPIRITS

Nothing captures the imagination more than the idea of elves and fairies. In our rationalistic search for greater knowledge, however, we have grown less sensitive to the nuances of nature. We no longer see with either the child's eyes or those of the seer. Instead we laugh and scoff at those who do.

It is easy to think we know all about the world as explorers have touched all four corners. Still, the myths and tales of mysterious realms and lands fascinate. Many of our myths and legends are based in fact which is why they still intrigue us.

As we open our awareness to life that exists on all levels, we will be drawn into contact with the more ethereal realms of life. These lands have gone by many names—Eden, Hesperides, Avalon, etc. As we begin our quest for contact with the spirit realms of life, we will follow in the footsteps of those whose paths have been recorded in our myths and tales.

The call of the quest is a call to adventure and excitement. It is not usually seen for what it really is—a time of maturing and growth. One of the goals of any quest is the entering into a state of new and higher perception.

Our quest into the spirit realms of life will bring contact with those beings of nature who fascinate and stir our imagination. The elves and fairies of lore serve a vital and creative function in life, and as we expand our perceptions we will come to know them.

People all over the world believe in rare creatures and beings, both superior and inferior to humans. Those we call the elves and fairies have many differing claims to their origins. Some sources claim they are simply the spirits of the dead. Other sources see them as a remnant of a race more ancient than humanity. Others claim they are simply part of the angelic kingdom.

There is, in fact, much information about them, although little of it can be verified. Literature, songs, mystics and clairvoyants have been the traditional sources. The truth, though, is that their world is only as far away as we allow it to be.

Nature spirits are Mother Earth's children. They are as many-sided as nature itself. They come in many shapes and sizes. Because their energy is not as physical as ours, they have the ability to work on many dimensions. Although most classify all of the nature spirits as elves or fairies, we should avoid this. They are as diverse as humanity, but like humanity they do have much in common.

Almost all nature spirits require some contact with humans. Many require the direct assistance of humanity to live and evolve. They affect us as much as we affect them. Unfortunately, the human abuses of nature —of the physical world and of each other— appalls and affects them. It forces an increasing withdrawal from contact with humanity. Not all are able to withdraw, however. Some are bound to suffer the consequences of human behavior. For this reason, and although it may require great effort, it is important to establish greater understanding, contact and rapport with them.

The Habitats of the Nature Spirits

It is believed that fairies and elves cannot be perceived by vulgar eyes. In spite of this, their habitats are uniformly described in most societies. Their habitats have gone by many names: the Western Isles, Tir Nan Og, Avalon, Land of the Forever Young, Em Hain, Island of Women, Neverland, Middle Earth, etc. They live everywhere and nowhere. They are always in woodlands and fields. The traditional concept of them living within hollow trees is more fact than fiction.

The nature spirits can be found in caves, across rivers, underwater, around lakes, between bushes, and within trees. They are found in all manifestations of nature. Fairy mounds are raised areas upon the ground, indicating their habitats. Fairy rings are areas of grass marked with a perimeter of some kind.

The pathways and habitats of the nature spirits will again become more recognizable as you begin to expand your own perceptions. You will find that certain nature spirits will be easier for you to perceive than others. Some individuals find them more recognizable in waterways. I have no trouble seeing them in trees and bushes. As you work with them, you will find the area of nature in which your perception of them is the easiest.

Generally distrustful of humans, they are not quick to reveal themselves. Spend as much time in nature as you can. When you do begin to perceive them it is often as a glimmer or hint just at the edge of your vision. Although they will blend and shape-shift themselves into different forms, with a keen eye and persistence you will begin to recognize them in their natural habitats. You may see faces in shrubs or flowers and assume it's the light or your imagination. If you do not see them, being out in nature will help you to at least feel their presence. This feeling is often like walking through a spider web while in the middle of a field.

One group of these beings is called the *Flower Fairies*. These are always active in areas where there are flowers, wild and domestic. These are "Tinkerbelle" kinds of beings. They are always drawn to children, especially those who are playing outside.

There are elves and fairies found mainly within field environments. Some, who are called *Fauni* and *Silvani*, are wood sprites. They are abundant in forests.

Rock and stone spirits are also common, more so than most of us imagine. The popularity of crystals has drawn many new individuals into contact with this group. In every crystal and stone is a deva or nature spirit who works with it. The rock and stone spirits have a great antiquity about them, and a great strength. Stone devas can be found in any major rock formation. The stone spirits are believed by some to hold the keys to prophecy, magic and the knowledge of secret treasures.

The tree spirits have a great lore about them. They are living beings. Every tree has its own spirit or deva. This spirit can emerge from the tree for short distances and for brief periods of times. They are usually more active at night because they are not as active helping the tree grow during this time. This greater activity at night makes people more susceptible to actually feeling their energy. This can be experienced as chills, an uneasy feeling, etc. This is also why many people are uncomfortable in a forest at night.

Tree spirits can't harm us, but their energies are strong and different. Contact with them can cause chills and shivers. Willow spirits have a habit of following travelers on dark nights, muttering and making noises behind the wanderer. You should not be frightened of this. It is much more amusing than it is sinister.

Tree spirits can be quite affectionate to people. This is often why some individuals have a favorite tree in which they find great comfort and balance. A blue spruce in the front of our home appeared to be dead when we first moved in. Within the first month it was alive, full and shimmering with life. I think it was simply lonely for human contact. It has been a great comfort and protection to our home.

Trees also house elf populations. Different kinds of elves and fairies attach themselves to different kinds of trees. They are very protective of their trees for they are tied to them for life. We must be careful in cutting down the trees, not only for ecological reasons, but because we can displace great numbers of these rare beings.

The home in which I now live had been left untended for over a year before it was purchased. The trees, shrubs and grasses were wild in the back yard. Without thinking, I decided to cut everything out and start from scratch. The shrubs ended up being tremendously difficult to cut down, although they should have been easy to remove.

It is now a great struggle to make anything grow in the areas I cut. Later, in one of the first meditations in this new home, I discovered the reason for this. I had cut down the homes of many nature spirits, displacing them.

Since then I have had to learn the lesson of how difficult it is and how much energy it takes for the nature spirits to make anything grow. It has been difficult rebuilding their trust during the past seven years. The nature spirits, though, have returned, and they make themselves more known. Now, before I do any cutting or trimming, I ask their permission and give them warning.

Of all the trees, the elder is believed to have the highest elf population, with many tiny elves living under its roots. It is known as a shelter to good fairies and elves and as a protection against evil spirits. The oak has been the object of much fairy lore and veneration. It is believed that the oak greatly resents being cut. Elms are believed to mourn the cut members of their family. The hawthorne has always been considered a fairy tree. Uprooting it is supposed to bring misfortune.

Although mostly inhabiting areas of nature, it is not uncommon to find nature spirits taking up residence under and in human dwellings. Usually these entities like being around homes with children and where there is lots of activity. They are tireless and filled with energy. They can and do assist in the smooth running of the house. They can also be mischievous. Tradition says that they should not be paid—especially with clothing—or they leave forever. This was reflected in the old fairy tale of the "Shoemaker and the Elves."

Occasionally, *dark elves* will take up residence in the homes of humans. They prefer dark corners of rooms. They usually only appear at night. They are not dangerous or harmful and they can stimulate great craftsmanship. Their energy is strong. Many more people have felt their presence than realize it.

My mother would do the laundry in the basement when I was growing up, and it was interesting to watch how my brothers (and myself) would act when asked to retrieve it. The light would be flipped on, but it was never enough. We would go calmly down the stairs and begin gathering the clothes in our arms. By the time the clothes were gathered the uneasiness of being down there was hitting. The eyes would look about, searching the shadows. Then we would bolt up the stairs on tip toe (trying to disguise our hasty exit). We would pause at the door to calm ourselves and pretend we had just casually walked up the stairs, completely unbothered.

Many have had these same feelings and experiences in their own homes. These kinds of feelings are stimulated not just by superstitious fears. Often it indicates the presence of a dark elf. Their energy affects our feeling nature. It can cause chills and shivers and a definite feeling of uneasiness or of a presence.

Often the spirits of nature speak to us without our realizing it. Have you ever taken a walk and caught a whiff of pine as you passed the tree? Did you ever catch the fragrance of a flower while those you may be walking with did not? Did a tree rustle on a still day as you passed beneath it? Was there a ripple in a pond or a creek just as you sat down beside it? These are the nature spirits reaching out and speaking to you.

The spirits of nature are found in all elements of nature—earth, stone, water, air, and even in the deep fires of the earth. Their presence and touch is soft and subtle. If you wish to begin your search for the fairy realms, open to the elements of nature that are closest to you. Look around you, because even if you are not aware of them, the likelihood of their presence within your life is great.

Elementals and Nature Spirits

There is often confusion over the difference between the elementals and the nature spirits—the ones more commonly referred to as elves and fairies. Most people link them together as either nature spirits or as elementals, but there is a difference. They are all of the same hierarchy (angelic), but they serve different functions at different levels.

Those of the nature spirit level are more likely to display "personality," and the elementals have more of a "characteristic." For example, in any one family there may be a particular characteristic or trait that all of the family members have—a tendency to baldness, thinness, a sharp nose, etc. Each person in that family, though, will display a unique personality, despite the common characteristic.

Elementals are the building blocks of nature. They are close to being true energy and consciousness. When we are in contact with them they will stimulate strong responses in us. Learning to work with the elementals is a way of attuning to all of the energies and beings of nature.

Elementals are four-dimensional. They have nothing to obstruct their movements. Therefore, they move as easily through matter as we do air. They do require some contact with humans for their own evolution. Helping to direct them is an overseer, traditionally called the King of the element. The archangels oversee the activities of the kings, and each king oversees the activities of a group of elementals and nature spirits. Everything is hierarchical in the evolutionary scheme.

The Hierarchical Scheme

Element	Elemental Being	King	Overseeing Archangel
Earth	Gnomes	Ghob	Auriel
Water	Undines	Niksa	Gabriel
Air	Sylphs	Paralda	Raphael
Fire	Salamanders	Djin	Michael
Ether	——	——	Christ

The fifth element of Ether is the element from which came forth the other four. It has never been truly defined in some of the above categories. It encompasses aspects of all the other elements and the beings of those elements.

There are four main levels of elemental beings:

Gnomes (earth elementals)—

This is a generic title. It should not be confused with our usual conception of the gnome. Their form and shape is "earthy" in nature. They cannot fly and they can be burned in fire. They grow old in much the same manner as humans. Various types of entities fall into this category, each with its own degree of consciousness. They maintain and work with the physical structure of the earth. Gnomes help create color within our world and our lives.

They assist us in tying into the earth energies and in understanding how to use those hidden forces.

They also work to maintain the physical body of humans—its composition, its assimilation of minerals, etc. Without them we could not function in the physical world. One earth elemental is usually assigned to help us maintain our physical vehicles. As with many elementals, it is through their association and work with humans that they can become ensouled and evolve. They are affected by what we do. If we abuse the body, we abuse the elemental assigned to us.

The gnomes are needed to build the plants, flowers and trees. It is their task to tint them, to make the minerals and crystals and to maintain the earth so that we have a place to grow and evolve. They are the beings of craftsmanship.

The gnomes guard the treasures of earth and are attuned to helping humans find the treasures within the earth or part of it. This can be hidden treasure, the energy of a crystal or stone, or finding the gold within one's life. They help keep us rational and grounded, so it is good to connect with them regularly—especially at those times we seem to become more flighty.

They work with humans through nature. They give each stone its own individuality —its own energy. They do this with every aspect of nature. Thus we can learn from each one. Every tree, rock and flower has something that it can teach us.

Undines (water elementals)—

This is a classification for those beings associated with the water element. Wherever there is a natural source of water they can be found. All water upon the planet—rain, river, ocean, etc.—has tremendous undine activity. They, like the gnomes, are also subject to mortality, but they are more enduring.

The undines work to maintain the astral body of humans and to stimulate our feeling nature. This is associated with heightened psychic feelings as well as emotional ones. Theirs is the energy of creation, birth and intuition.

An undine is also assigned to each of us to help with the function of our bodily fluids—blood, lymphatic fluids, etc. Abuse of our body abuses them, and once assigned they can only endure. They are dependent upon humans for growth. As we evolve, so do they.

Diseases of the blood contaminate them, and many of the modern diseases such as AIDS, which effects bodily fluids, ties the undine to the karma and the effects of the disease, no matter how unwilling they may be. Water is the springwell of life, and these beings are essential to our finding that springwell within. They are essential to the gifts of empathy, healing and purification.

The undines are usually female in form although there are mermen, too. They work with humans to help us discover our beauty —both outer and inner. They work with us to help us realize that our beauty comes from what we do and not from what we look like.

Undines also stimulate strong emotions and creativity in humans. They assist us in absorbing and assimilating life experiences so that we can use them to the fullest. They can help us to see and feel the fullest ecstasy of the creative acts of life, be it sexual, artistic or the performance of a duty with the right emotion.

They often work with us through our dreams. Dreams of water and sensuality often reflect undine activity—their stimulation of us to greater creativity in our lives. Work with them can assist us in strengthening the astral body for full, conscious, out-of-body experiences.

Sylphs (air elementals)—

The sylphs are probably more closely in line with our concept of fairies and angels than the other elemental beings. They work side-by-side with the angels. They are part of the creative element of air. It is their work which results in the tiniest of breezes to the mightiest tornadoes.

Not all of the sylphs are restricted to living in the air. Most are of high intelligence. Some have much to do with humans, often helping to alleviate pain and suffering and stimulate inspiration and creativity. One of their special tasks is to help children who have just passed over. They also serve as temporary guardian angels until we open ourselves and draw to us the one who will be *the holy guardian angel*.

A sylph is also assigned to each individual human. This sylph helps us to maintain our mental body. Thus, our thoughts (good or bad) are what most affects them. They work within us for the assimilation of oxygen from the air we breathe and with all functions of air in and around us. Exposure to pollution, smoking, etc. affects their appearance and alters their effectiveness in our lives.

Sylphs help to stimulating new knowledge and inspiration. They work to cleanse and uplift our thoughts and our intelligence. When you breathe deeply and notice a sweet freshness in the air, you are acknowledging their work.

The sylphs work with us to assist in using the intuitive and the rational together. Although often showing themselves in humanlike form, they are very much asexual. In fact, they often inspire this in others. In my experience, people with strong sylph activity often find that sexuality is not high on their list of priorities, and they may not understand how it can be so with others. The sylphs stimulate expression of the creative sexual drive into other avenues of one's life, such as work, etc.

Sylphs are also good to work with for protection of home and property. Their energy can be so strong that they make intruders confused or worried about entering your environment.

Salamanders (fire elementals)—

These are not to be confused with the reptile salamanders, although they have the same name. They are also found everywhere. No fire is lit without their help. Mostly they are active underground and internally within the body and mind. They are responsible for lightning, explosions and volcanoes.

Salamanders evoke powerful emotional currents in humans. They also stimulate fires of spiritual idealism and perception. Their energy assists in the tearing down of the old and the building up of the new, as fire is both destructive and constructive in its creative expression.

They also function in the physical body. They aid in circulation and in maintaining proper body temperature. They work with the body's metabolism for greater health. A slow metabolism is often an indication of sluggish salamander activity within the body. A high metabolism is an indication of great salamander activity in the body as well.

Salamanders have a great love for music, but they are foremost an agent of nature. Their energies are very stirring, and it takes tremendous ability to control and direct them for the most creative results. One who is a composer or poet, or in any way works with the creative power of words, could do worse than to attune to the fire elementals.

Fire elementals work with humans via heat, fire and flame. This includes everything from the flame of a candle to the ethereal flames and light of the sun on a daily basis. They can be powerfully effective in healing work including detoxifying the body, especially in critical situations. They must be used carefully in such times, as their energies are dynamic and difficult to control. They are almost always present when there is any healing going to occur.

The fire elementals can help awaken in us higher spiritual vision and aspiration. They strengthen and stimulate the entire auric field so that there is easier attunement to and recognition of higher spiritual forces within our lives.

We are more likely to have rapport with some elementals than others. It is important to understand and determine this. If we do we can more easily open the doors to inner realm perception. How do we determine which elementals we are more likely to harmonize with? There are two very simple ways.

The first is through astrology. Every astrological sign is associated with one of the four main elements of earth, water, air or fire. The birth sign reflects those energies you hope to unfold in this lifetime. The element of that sign reflects which element you also wish to unfold and develop. The beings of the element will assist you in that process, and thus you will be more able to attune and work with them. This does not mean you will be unable to attune and work with the others, rather it simply says that because of this link you will find that these will be the easiest for you to connect with.

The second is through identifying the major element in your first name. The vowels within our name, as illustrated in the chart below, are an excellent guide.

Vowel	Element	Elemental Beings
A*	Ether	All four groups of elementals
I	Fire	Salamanders
E	Air	Sylphs
O	Water	Undines
U	Earth	Gnomes

As before, the primary vowel (the one which is most strongly accented when pronounced) indicates which group you will align with most easily. Other vowels indicate other groups that they are secondary in ease of relating to them.

---

*For further information on the ether element and the vowel "A" (as well as the other vowels) consult the author's book, *The Sacred Power in Your Name* (St. Paul: Llewellyn Publications, 1990).

Those who have a vowel that aligns them with the ether element have a greater responsibility. This element gives wider access to all of the elemental kingdoms and an increased ability to work with them. There is also an increased ability to be affected by them.

If the element of astrology and the element of your name are the same, it may indicate that you have come to double your work with that group of beings. If they are opposite, it does not mean that they cancel themselves out. All elements and all elemental beings work well with each other. Use the charts on the following pages to understand the role of the elemental beings in your own life.

When working with these charts you should keep in mind that the ether element accentuates the aspects of whatever element it is associated with. It will enhance—or has the capability of enhancing—both the positive and negative aspects.

By following these instructions you will find that the process of opening the door to your elemental kingdom is easy:

1. Find a place out in nature that will reflect your element. If it is earth, find a secluded spot with rocks and where you can sit, feel-

Vowel and Astrological Elements

Element:	FIRE
Vowel:	I
Zodiacal Signs:	Aries, Leo, Sagittarius
Qualities of Elements:	Courage, self-assertive, visionary, helpful, creative expression, strong, active life force, imposing, fanatic, self-indulgent, authoritarian
Works with:	Salamanders

Element:	EARTH
Vowel:	U
Zodiacal Signs:	Taurus, Virgo, Capricorn
Qualities of Elements:	Providing necessities, grounded, good sense of timing, stable, self-aware, understands emotions, miserly, controlling, coarse, no empathy
Works with:	Gnomes

Element:	AIR
Vowel:	E
Zodiacal Signs:	Gemini, Libra, Aquarius
Qualities of Elements:	Mental, inventive, intelligent, quick, alert, cooperative, humane, cold, aloof, imitative, nervous, superficial
Works with:	Sylphs

Element:	WATER
Vowel:	O
Zodiacal Signs:	Cancer, Scorpio, Pisces
Qualities of Elements:	Understanding, emotions, psychic, sensitive, artistic, romantic, reserved, impressionable, self-indulgent, exaggerates feelings, sensual
Works with:	Undines

Element:	ETHER
Vowel:	A
Zodiacal Signs:	Ether is the substance from which all was created
Qualities of Elements:	Ether is the spiritual aspect that overrides and influences all elements. It permeates all creation.
Works with:	All

Differences of opinion exist as to the vowel associations of the earth and ether elements. These are guidelines. What is most important is how you associate and what correspondences *you* build. The author has used the "U" for the earth element as it also is a vowel whose sound correlates to the functions of the base chakra. The "A" is assigned to the ether because of its connection to the heart chakra which mediates all energies of the body, just as ether mediates the energies of all the elements.

Elemental Combinations

Combined Elements: Fire with Fire
Qualities & Relationships: Tremendous impulse and
stimulation; can burn self out; must find practical outlet; provides much energy toward life goal;
must balance self-expression.

Combined Elements: Air with Air
Qualities & Relationships: Excessively mental; not
enough direction; whirlpool of ideas needing
practical release; talkative and expressive.

Combined Elements: Water with Water
Qualities & Relationships: Can give added depth; increased sensitivity; feelings easily hurt; intoler-
ance; can lead to instability; requires a realistic
focus.

Combined Elements: Earth with Earth
Qualities & Relationships: Needs stimulus to manifest
latent fruit; can cause inertia; materialistic; must
work on self-expression and personal relationships;
stabilizing; latent talents.

Combined Elements: Fire with Earth
Qualities & Relationships: Learning boundaries of the
activity of fire; practicalize high ideals; inspiring
greater mobility; can ground the fire or stimulate expression.

Combined Elements: Fire with Air
Qualities & Relationships: Very compatible; too much air and fire is out of control; fire can change properties of air for good or bad; strengthens and raises ideals.

Combined Elements: Fire with Water
Qualities & Relationships: Fire turns water to steam; water puts out fires; when balanced they bring useful ideas/tremendous activity; alchemical processes are to be learned.

Combined Elements: Earth with Air
Qualities & Relationships: Air stimulates earth qualities; fruit needs oxygen; earth stabilizes volatile air aspects.

Combined Elements: Earth with Water
Qualities & Relationships: Very compatible as the two are necessary for anything to grow; earth stabilized the restless water element and water prevents dryness and unfeeling nature.

Combined Elements: Air with Water
Qualities & Relationships: Air keeps water fresh; water element can feel unfulfilled by air not understanding the emotions; intellect modifies oversensitivity; water broadens sympathies of air.

ing the earth. If it is water, sit by a stream or pond. If it is air, pick a day that has a breeze. If it is fire, sit where you can be in the sun.

2. Make sure you will not be disturbed in your spot. Relax. Perform the Mystic Marriage Exercise.

3. Softly tone the archangel's name for your element three times. Do it syllable by syllable as described in the last chapter. Use "The Hierarchical Scheme" chart in this chapter to identify the archangel for your element. As you do the toning, visualize yourself surrounded by the color of the archangel.

4. Pause and then softly tone the name of the king of your element three times. Give each syllable equal emphasis. See the color become stronger around you.

Element	King	Pronunciation
Earth	Ghob	(Gohb)
Water	Niksa	(Nihk-Suh)
Air	Paralda	(Pah-Rahl-Dah)
Fire	Djin	(Jihn)

5. Softly sound or sing your name outward three times.

6. Now tone the primary vowel sound. As you inhale, sound it silently. As you exhale, sound it audibly. Do this slowly and comfortably. Visualize this as a call to the elementals.

7. Extend your senses outward. Feel and sense the energies around you. Open your eyes slowly and take in the scene of nature around you. This exercise lets them know that you are ready to work with them more consciously. Allow yourself to be impressed with how best to use their energies constructively throughout the rest of the day.

Medieval magicians learned to call upon and use the elementals to help create and materialize fantastic creatures for various purposes. It was not uncommon for these magicians to use these etheric dragons to guard and protect their homes. These could, of course, be fire dragons, water dragons, earth dragons, air dragons or any combination.

Understanding Fairy Behavior

There is much more to the fairy realm than we often realize. They are not evil as some would believe, but they can be very mischievous. Their energies can also be very stimulating, and can even induce altered states of consciousness.

Pixies were often blamed for travelers becoming lost. They can become invisible, and their energy is so strong that they can confuse the senses, causing a traveler to miss a familiar marker. This intense energy, when in their natural surroundings, creates an altered state of consciousness (a "feeling dazed" effect). Thus a traveler may not notice his or her surroundings. Travelers are often mislead out of sheer mischief.

Turning one's coat inside out was believed to counter this dazed effect caused by pixies. This behavior actually forces the mind to its normal state of consciousness.

There are different powers according to the different types of nature spirits. They all vary in their ability to affect humans and human conditions. Almost all of the nature spirits have no true means of offense. For their defense against humans they have other abilities. These include levitation, shape-shifting, glamour, invisibility, etc. Some hold the secrets to great healing and to great treasures in the earth. Some are master craftspeople. Some have the gift of music, and others have the ability to bestow good or ill luck.

All fairies, elves, gnomes, elementals and

other nature spirits have the ability to reveal themselves in a physical form if they so desire. They will often take the form that people expect to see.

There are certain taboos associated with nature spirit contact. If you wish to work with them you should be careful not to break these taboos. To talk about a fairy or a fairy gift in a bad manner will cause them to withdraw. Denying the fairy or a gift from the fairies will also push them away and can result in a temporary string of bad luck. To reveal the presence of a fairy or the reality of a fairy gift when it is supposed to be a secret is considered poor ethics.

How do we know a fairy gift when we receive one? Fairies often show kindness to humans, especially their favorites. They repay acts of kindness to nature through a series of good luck events. The individual may encounter an unexpected source of prosperity. In the spiritualist seance room, *apports* (gifts from spirit) may be given with the aid of elementals which help them to materialize. These include special stones, shells, flowers, etc. Apports usually have special significance for the individual.

While out walking you may be greeted by a lovely fragrance. This can be a fairy gift to you from the flower fairy. You may find a feather in your path. This may be a gift from a sylph to help you connect with them more strongly. You may have someone give you a crystal or stone out of the blue. This may be a gift from the gnome kingdom. Someone may hug you or compliment you, all as a result of the influence from the undine kingdom.

The nature spirits teach us not to take things for granted. They teach us to appreciate them. We should honor such occasions and give thanks for them—regardless of their source (fairy or otherwise). Meditating upon them can provide much insight into the source of such occasions.

Those of the nature realm do have an ethics about them. Among themselves they maintain a high standard of loyalty. They dislike babblers and those who betray secrets. They also dislike those who disrespect nature in any manner—purposely or otherwise. They also dislike an explicit "thanks" for a fairy gift, but appreciation can be shown. They rarely take oaths, for nothing is detested so much as lies. They hold in great distaste human ambition, slovenliness, infidelity and inconstancy. They are also known for their amorousness and their ability to stimulate it in humans.

Those of the fairy realm do have the ability to bestow great gifts. These are often called *patronesses*. This is similar to the "fairy godmothers" of lore. These are usually spirits of great age and power. The *Fees* and the *White Ladies* are the two most common patronesses. Both seemed to disappear, but they are promised to return in the 20th century. Both are always very helpful to humans and very generous. When you have encountered one your life makes a wonderful turn around.

The Fees are considered the oldest beings on the planet. It is from them that we get the traditional image of the fairy godmother with a blue ball gown and a magic wand. Their advice should always be followed to the letter. When they borrow something, they always return it with a blessing. They can be found in every corner of nature.

The White Ladies are also very ancient and highly evolved. They usually are only seen when they kiss a child, blessing it, or when you are alone and out in nature. When the latter instance occurs, you may simply encounter an old woman strolling through nature who pauses to greet you. Then when you turn around, you will find that no one is there. This is often the first touch and the opening of the door to the White Lady Blessing.

Fairy Patronesses are always beautiful, but they are dwindling in number. They have certain demands which they place upon the protégés they choose. First is that the protege be free and open. The protege should always be generous in dealing with others. This they often test. The protege should be hospitable and truthful in word and deed. You should be courteous and ready to perform a kindness. They also expect you to be straightforward.

There are many easy ways of drawing the nature spirits closer to you. Show respect for all of Mother Nature. Learn to recognize and work with the elementals working with you. Take frequent walks in nature and show appreciation for it. Leave an area of your yard to grow wild for the fairies and nature spirits to play in and work with in the manner they choose. Involve yourself in a creative or artistic endeavor. They are always drawn to such activities. You don't have to be expert at them, just freely and joyfully participate. Sing often. They gather wherever there is song and music, especially when it is simple and comes from the heart.

8

HONORING OUR SPIRIT TOTEMS

There is a growing involvement in shamanism. The shamans and priests of ancient societies were the keepers of the sacred knowledge. They were tied to the rhythms and forces of nature. They were able to walk the threads that link the visible and invisible worlds.

Part of the shamanic tradition involves our reconnecting to the energies of the earth and all life upon it. "Once every people in the world believed that the trees were divine and could take a human or grotesque shape and dance among the shadows; and that deer and ravens and foxes and wolves and ears and clouds and pools, almost all things under the sun and moon, were not less divine and changeable."*

---

* Stephen Larsen, The Shaman's Doorway. (New York: Harper and Row, 1976).

A totem is any natural object, being or animal with whose phenomena and energy you feel closely associated during your life. Although we will focus more upon spirit guides working through animal totems, they also work through the energies of objects. Some will reflect energies operating for only short times, and some are with us from birth to death and beyond.

We can use the animal imagery and other totem images as a way to learn about ourselves and the invisible world. We do not have to believe that these images and totems are beings of great intelligence, but there is an archetypal power that resides behind and oversees these creatures. These archetypes have their own qualities and characteristics which are reflected through the behaviors and activities of specific animals.

When we honor the totem animal we are honoring the essence that lies behind it. We are opening and attuning to that essence. We then share its power or its medicine in our life. The animal is a symbol of a specific force of the invisible realm which manifests within the physical world. By studying the animal or totem, and then merging with it, we become able to call its energy forth whenever needed. This brings to us those beings of the spirit realm which also work with that energy.

There was a time when humanity recognized itself as part of nature and nature as part of it. Dreaming and waking were inseparable realities; the natural and the supernatural merged and blended. People used the images of nature to express this unity and to reinstill a transpersonal kind of experience. This is seen in the wearing of skins and feathers as is common in many Amerindian and aboriginal societies.

Adopting the guise of animals—wearing skins or masks—symbolized a reawakening and endowing oneself with certain energies. Nature totems are symbols of fertility and life. Each species has its own power to remind us what we can manifest within our own life. The animal becomes a spirit guide. It helps us to bridge the natural world to the supernatural. It awakens the realities of both.

Animals have had much strong symbology associated with them. They have represented the emotional life of humanity, reflecting qualities that must be overcome, controlled and/or re-expressed. They are also symbols of powers—powers of the often invisible realms that we could learn to manifest within the visible.

The Masked Sorcerer

A prevalent symbol associated with Shamanism, its image is taken from a prehistoric cave painting. Early man, surrounded by mysterious forces, responded to them through imitation. Man attempted to bring the divine into accord with the will of humanity. Priests used totems and images to assist in coming face-to-face with the mystery. Through dance, costume, etc. the priest or priestess would take complete identity with the deity and its powers. This is the symbol of the prophet, medicine person and the manifestation of the powers of nature. Images such as this invoke a presence which helps one to transcend the physical. Wearing the skins of the animal was a means of appeasing its spirit and honoring its power.

Birds were often symbols of the soul. Their ability to fly reflects the ability within us to rise to new awareness. It reflects the ability to bridge the physical world with the heavens. As totems, they each have their own peculiar characteristics, but they all can be used to align us with spirit guides who stimulate inspiration, hope and ideas.

Aquatic life can also be a totem. Water is a symbol of the astral plane experience and the creative element of life. Various fish and other forms of aquatic life symbolize the guidance that comes from our intuitive or feminine side. Those guides who work through these images will help us to awaken that aspect.

Insects are a part of nature and can also be spirit totems. Michael Harner warns against their use, but they have a strong symbology associated with them. From the bee of fertility in Egyptian myths to the Mantis of the African bushmen and the many tales of the Spider Woman who created the universe, they are as much a part of working with spirit totems as any animal.

By studying and reading about the animals, birds, fish and insects, you can learn much about the qualities and characteristics of the guide that is working with you through that image. You also will learn much about which qualities this guide will help you to unfold. Keep in mind that each species has its own powers. An ant may not seem as glamourous as a bear totem, but it is industrious and it has a strength that far exceeds its size, a strength that, proportionately, the bear does not have.

> *If you talk to the animals*
> *they will talk with you*
> *and you will know each other.*
> *If you do not talk to them,*
> *you will not know them,*
> *And what you do not know*
> *you will fear.*
> *What one fears*
> *one destroys.*

—Chief Dan George

Meeting Your Spirit Totems

The shaman works to reconnect conscious human life with nature and spirit through the totem. The image of the animal helps us transcend our normal, waking consciousness so that we can more easily attune to other realms and beings. This begins with realizing that all inner vision and imagery has validity on some level.

What gets most people into trouble is the *interpretation* of the images. Reading, studying and learning about these images will facilitate relating them to ourselves. We don't have to accept the totem images without question. We can demand that our spirit guide energies be expressed to us in an image that we can relate to. If you are uncomfortable with an animal totem from your spirit guide after having put it through a verification process, simply send it on its way.

At the same time, the animal totems that you receive should not be haphazardly discarded simply because it is not as glamorous or as powerful as your ego wanted. Only study and exploration of that animal will reveal its significance to you. Searching out that significance is a way of honoring the totem. This helps build the bridge between your physical world and the spirit realm within it.

The meditation that follows is designed to assist you in discovering your spirit totem. It will begin the process of opening the spirit realm of nature as it relates to your life.

1. Begin by making sure you will be undisturbed. Take the phone off the hook, etc. Light any incense or use a fragrance that may help you in your meditation.

2. Perform your relaxation exercise. Follow this with the Mystic Marriage Exercise. Then simply visualize the scenes described below. If you wish, you may record them so that you can image and visualize along with the tape. Otherwise, read this several times, and familiarize yourself with it:

As you allow yourself to relax, pull your energies within yourself. You are going to go deep within yourself to discover the totem that lives within. This totem is a reflection of the spiritual energies that are working outside of you to help you in your life.

Imagine yourself standing in the midst of a wide field. The air is still and there is a calmness around you. It is dusk, that powerful time between day and night. The sun is still visible, although setting, and the moon is also visible in the sky. It is the time when day and night mingle, the time of the intersection of light and dark, physical and spirit.

Before you is a tall oak tree. Its bark is gnarled and twisted and its roots extend far into the heart of the earth itself. Its branches block the view of the sky as you stand beneath it. You are unable to see its uppermost branches.

There is a small opening at its base, just large enough to squeeze through if you bend over. With a last look over your shoulder toward the setting sun, you step into the inner darkness of the tree.

There is the smell of moss and moist wood. As you squeeze through the narrow opening you find that it widens as you mover further in. Soon you are able to stand erect, and you breathe a little easier. You pause, catching your breath and summoning your courage to move further inside.

It is then that you hear the sound.

At first it is faint—hardly discernible. You hold perfectly still to insure that the sound is not your own movement. The sound is soft, but as you move forward, feeling your way in the darkness of the tree, it grows louder. It is the sound of a distant drum. In the darkness of the inner tree, the drum's sound is hollow and primal. For a moment you imagine it as the heartbeat of the tree itself.

The beat is slow and regular. Its hollow tone touches the core of you. It coaxes you through the dark, and you go deeper within the heart of the tree itself. It is hypnotic. You know it is sounding forth what you have awaited a long time. You are not sure what it will be. You have never been sure, but you know you will recognize it when faced with it.

You continue forward, feeling your way, somehow knowing it is better to go forward than to return. You begin to notice that it is growing lighter. At first you think it is simply your eyes adjusting to the darkness. Then ahead of you, you see a torch burning which illuminates the path you are on. The path is narrow. Its sides are steep and ridged with the inner veins and arteries of the tree. You touch them. Surprisingly, they feel warm. You understand. Blood runs warmly through all living things. It is comforting.

You approach the torch and find it at the top of a steep, descending path. This path is illuminated by sporadically placed torches. You hesitate momentarily, and then begin your descent. You place your feet carefully, for the path is covered in spots slick with moss.

The illumination grows brighter with each step down the spiral path leading you into the inner heart of the planet. You feel as if you are following the roots of the tree to the core of the earth. You know that on some level you are being led to a primal point of life and energy within yourself.

The drumbeat has grown to a steady volume. It has become a part of your own rhythms and you have become a part of its. As you continue to wind downward another sound begins to touch you. It entices you even more deeply into the heart of the earth. It is the sound of running water—a stream or a waterfall—you are not sure which.

It is then that you see the end of your tunnel. Ahead is a large, cave-like opening. Beyond the opening you can see sunlight and the greens of nature. You can also see a river of crystalline water running through what seems to be the heart of the meadow. You step through the opening, and the drumming stops.

The sunshine warms and brightens you. It is as if you have stepped out of the womb of life. Wildflowers of every color and fragrance fill your senses with their beauty. The grasses are emerald green. At the edge of the meadow is a forest of rich dark green —the color of primeval life at its purest.

You move into the meadow. The warmth of the sun fills you with a fire that heals and soothes, chasing away any remaining fears. You fill your lungs with air that is sweet and fresh. It feels so good to just breathe.

You move to the edge of the river and watch as it flows over rocks, creating eddies and spirals of myriad shapes. The sun glints off its surface with rainbow hues. You look down the river and see that it leads to a distant ocean. All waters are here. You bend down and gently cup your hand into the river. You bring its cool sweet elixir to your mouth, quenching your thirst.

Next to the river is a large stone in the shape of a chair. Warmed by the sun, you settle into it. It fits your form perfectly. From here you can enjoy all of the elements of the meadow—the forests, the grasses, the distant ocean and the sky above. You are filled with a sense of peace. Here you can rediscover the power that is yours to claim in life.

As you look about you catch your breath. As if in response to your thoughts there is a movement. It may come from the forest, sky, distant ocean or it may be a combination.

You sit still watching as this totem moves closer to you. Its eyes seek you out and hold your gaze. Never have you seen anything so wonderful—so unique. Such life forms had always seemed so wild and out of touch, but there is no fear here. There is only recognition and wonder.

As if in response to this thought, the animal makes a sound, movement or gesture indicating its own unique power and strength. Then it disappears.

You stand up, looking about. It had happened so quickly. Had it all been your imagination? You scan the entire area, searching. Nothing is seen.

Had you done or thought something to offend it? You stand confused, unsure. It had been so beautiful, so noble, such a unique expression of life. It truly deserved to be honored and respected.

Again, as if in response to your thoughts, a trumpeting rings through the meadow. You turn towards the mouth of the cave. There in the darkness within is your totem. Its image freezes briefly, its eyes holding yours once more. Then it fades from view.

You smile and laugh, running toward the opening. You understand. As you give it honor and respect, its energies come alive for you and within you, serving as a guide between worlds. Its energies are yours to claim as your own, but they can only be claimed through honor, love and respect.

At the mouth of the cave lay a conch shell. A part of you knows—and long ignored—that this is a symbol of calling forth new energy. It is a symbol of the womb of life, and the trumpeting upon the conch shell is a reminder that life can be called forth on all realms.

You pick up the conch shell, your gift and reminder of the realms that touch you and live within you. You offer a silent prayer of gratitude and step back into the cave, leaving the meadow behind you.

It is now well lit and the path is wide and clear. In the distance you see the vague image of your newfound friend leading the way. Soon you see the light that leads you out of the tree itself.

As you step from the tree you see your totem retreating back within its depths. Now you understand that as you claim your own power and learn to work in all realms, the paths in all walks of life become clearer and more easily managed.

You cradle the conch shell in your arms and breathe deeply. The field and the large oak tree begin to fade, and you find yourself drawn back to the present in peace and in balance.

Honoring Your Spirit Totems

Part of the process of working with our totems involves honoring them. Hanging pictures, drawing pictures, reading and learning as much about their characteristics and behaviors are just some of the ways of doing so. The more we honor them—the more significance we give them in our lives—the more powerful and effective they become.

The totem discovered in the previous meditation serves as an excellent bridge to the spirit realm. It will give you greater power and strength in working with those more elusive and ethereal realms.

Do not be surprised if mythical creatures arise as totems. It is not uncommon. They often reflect spirit guides who are working to help us transcend normal states of consciousness.

As you discover your totems you will find that they come to you in dreams and meditations. You will encounter them in many ways, and these serve to confirm your experience.

You will come across pictures, postcards, curios in which a totem is depicted. You may find yourself discovering television programs exploring its habitats and behaviors with greater frequency. Books, myths and depictions of it will cross your path. You do not have to indulge in all of these, but by acknowledging them and taking advantage of them, you honor the spirit energies working in your life through that totem.

1. Learn as much about your spirit totem as possible. Read about it. Learn its basic

qualities, habits and behaviors. Research myths and tales associated with it. All of these will help you in understanding how best to use its energies in working with the spirit realm.

2. Find pictures and artwork of your totem. Make a collage of them encircling a picture of yourself.

3. Meditate upon the animal. Visualize it before you, speaking to you telepathically. Let it tell you how it can help in different areas of your life. Visualize it merging into you. Perform meditation where you see yourself as this totem.

4. Draw and sketch pictures of it. Artistic endeavors stimulate the right hemisphere of the brain. This helps us in our intuitive perceptions of the entire spirit realm.

5. Buy figurines of your totem. They do not have to be large or expensive.

6. Buy small tokens, images and such of your totem. Present them as gifts to family and friends. As you give the gift you are honoring the universality of spirit and its

ability to help everyone. You do not have to tell everyone why you are doing it. Nor do you have to explain its esoteric significance.

7. Give an anonymous donation to a wildlife fund or a specific organization associated with your totem animal. As you promote and protect the life of your totem, the spirit behind it will work to promote and protect yours. The anonymity ensures that the honoring is for the sake of honoring rather than for recognition.

Do not boast of what your totem does for you and others. Disbelief on the part of others, expressed or not, can hinder and restrict your connection to this totem spirit. There is strength in silence. Speaking of your relationship with your totem can dissipate its energies before it gets a chance to work some real magic for you.

There is nothing wrong with letting others know that you simply like or are fascinated with such animals. If anyone asks, simply tell them you admire its energy and qualities. A totem is personal. Yes, individuals may have the same generic kind of animal, but the manner in which it works for you will be unique and different from the way it works for someone else. It is neither better nor worse, just different.

We must learn to honor our relationships and allow them to unfold with respect. As you grow and unfold in your relationship with spirit, the way in which it works for you may also change. Be creative in this relationship and in your honoring of it. Give thanks to whatever divine source you worship for assisting you through this spirit totem.

9

DISCARNATES, GHOSTS AND HAUNTINGS

We have all heard the stories. The telephone rings. You pick it up and you hear a familiar voice. It is the voice of someone who has passed away.

There are many such ghost stories and strange occurrences. They have been the inspiration for TV, movies and books. But just what is the truth? Many have reported "ghostly experiences." Most often they simply want to know if their unusual experience was real or imaginary.

These experiences are not easily explained. There is often a lack of evidence and distortion because of the emotions that come into play. Of course, many ghostly experiences are explained with non-paranomral, conventional answers. But much is fact and can't be shoved aside.

There is a great deal of fear of death. This is natural. Humans always fear what they don't understand. Still, with all of this fear, the possibility of the personality existing after physical death is misunderstood, disbelieved and even scoffed at.

Ghosts have been perceived in many ways. They are seen as evil specters and demons. They have been depicted as cute and helpful. They have been described as trapped in the *nether world*, a home for the restless dead or lost souls. They are seen as simply passive and harmless. Ghostly hauntings of homes and other locations have ranged from evil to mischievous to harmless wanderings of a spirit who doesn't know where else to go or what to do.

All ghosts and all spirits are often bunched together under the category of evil specters and demons out to terrorize and frighten humans. This is the fodder for T.V., movies, and popular fiction. In actuality it has little to do with reality.

We need to begin our examination of this phenomena by defining the terms:

Apparition—

Apparition is a term usually designating any visible object or being of supernatural origin. They are most commonly considered to be the figures of someone dead or a long way off. It is a term used to imply a return of the entity to familiar surroundings to accomplish a particular goal. Apparition and ghost, as with all of these terms, are often used interchangeably.

Bogie Man—

A generic term used to encompass and describe any tormenting or frightening spirit. Most ghost stories center around this particular aspect, yet it is the rarest of ghosts. One form of bogie man was the *ankou*, the graveyard watcher. In parts of Europe, when a new graveyard was created, it was customary to bury an unfortunate victim alive in the first grave so that a ghostly guardian was created. This tormented soul would frighten off others—alive or dead—so that the peace of the departed would not be disturbed.*

Discarnate—

Discarnates are the same as ghosts. They are beings without bodies: they are incorporeal. Discarnate often implies a more recently passed on human soul.

---

* Peter Haining, *Dictionary of Ghost Lore.* (Englewood Cliffs: Prentice-Hall, 1984), p. 6.

Ghost—

Ghost is a name usually applied to the visible spirit of a person who has died. We will use it in this book to represent the soul of a dead person—a disembodied spirit. There can be animal ghosts. Many people have seen apparitions of a favorite pet after it has died. This pet may walk through the home, leave warm spots on a bed or chair it usually slept in, etc.

Poltergeist—

Literally, it means a "noisy ghost." It is a ghost that makes disturbances and otherwise unexplained noises. There is a debate as to whether they actually exist. Poltergeist activity occurs most often in homes where there is an adolescent girl. It is believed that as the young girl enters puberty, a tremendous amount of psychic energy is released. Many believe that it is simply this psychic energy being released that creates the phenomena, while others defend the idea that this new energy activates and draws the troublesome spirits.

Spirit—

A spirit can be any being that lives, works and operates on a non-physical level. This includes our guides, the angelic hierarchy, nature spirits and the souls of those who have passed on from the physical life.

Every society has had its own way of classifying and naming spirits and ghosts. Some of the more ancient have even tried to describe in intricate detail what the soul goes through after death. These writings include elaborate rituals and descriptions of the afterlife. Two of the more famous are the Egyptian and Tibetan Books of the Dead.

The truth is that experiences with spirits are not limited to the seance room of a medium, to old castles or to times past. Most people have had or will have some experience with this phenomena. Something will be seen when there is nothing there. A voice will be heard, again with no one present. A feeling of someone standing beside or behind you will be felt. The face of a loved one who has passed on may be seen behind a reflection in a mirror. A family picture will be developed and the face of a deceased loved one will appear in it. The apparition of a loved one who has passed on will reveal itself to comfort those who remain here.

When the incident occurs, it is not to be feared. Rather, it should be embraced with joy and wonder. It should awaken the reality of life on all planes, and it should affirm that we are never truly separate from the ones we love.

The common conception of ghosts as spirits of the dead staying close to the earth should be somewhat comforting to us. Many times, family members who pass away will stay close to the earth to serve as spirit guides to other family members. They may be recognized through touches, fragrances and even actual appearances. My own grandfather comes to me at times. He is always preceded by the smell of heavy tobacco. It was a fragrance that was common to the room in the house he shared with us growing up.

Those which we call ghosts—the essences of those who walked the earth—can do much for us. They show us that there is truly no such thing as death. They comfort us in our time of loss. They often return at different times throughout our lives to provide guidance, appearing to us in dreams and meditations. Yes, we must be careful about calling them up all of the time—they have their own lives to continue with on other dimensions. At the same time, though, they serve as guides through death and all of the fears we have about it.

Death is the great mystery of life. Part of our fear of it comes from believing it separates us from those we love. Because of this, many souls will remain earthbound to soothe and strengthen mourners and those seriously affected by the transition. Sometimes they remain behind to inspire certain actions or thoughts in the minds of intimate associates. And sometimes souls remain earthbound to help untangle any mysteries and to pass on any final messages.

Those who loved us in life do not stop loving us in death. Often the soul of a deceased loved one will return, if only briefly, to confirm this for us. Although startling, they should never frighten us. Such occasions should be embraced with joy.

Most funeral customs have a hidden aspect that is linked to the concept of life after death. As the soul untangles its energy from the physical body it is separated from the normal *prana* or life force that it would draw through the physical body. Thus it draws energy from other sources. This is why flowers are placed about and candles are lit.

Many people avoid funerals because of the strange feelings associated with them. These feelings come from several sources. As the soul withdraws from the physical, so does the archangel which watches over that soul. This creates a definite feeling of emptiness.

Another source of these feelings comes from the fact that no soul passes unaided. The presences of others who have passed will draw closer. Friends, relatives and loved ones no longer in the physical will gather to assist the deceased soul and to help provide comfort to those still in the physical.

The elementals are also very active during the death and funeral process. Their energy is always strong and often tangible. They are always present when organic matter needs to be animated or disintegrated.

Although the color black is considered the death color, it is very insulating. It protects and prevents oversensitivity to those subtle energies at funerals.

So what of communication with those who have passed on? Some consider it harmless, while others consider the attempt to communicate with them harmful to both the living and the deceased. As in most things, a balance between the two is probably more correct. As long as the deceased live in our memory there is a psychic rapport. As long as they live in our memory and we feel emotion, we are in touch with them. We are affecting them, and they are affecting us. There must be caution about trying to continually call them up through a medium because the deceased do not get to do what they need to do in other realms if they are distracted by us.

Much evidence exists to back the possibility of minds or personalities living after physical death. From Washington, D.C. to the Pacific coast, ghosts are found to exist. Traditional ghosts still live in old homes in Europe and America, but they also are found in southern mansions, modern two-story houses and just about any style of home.

There are houses with footsteps, doors opening and furniture being arranged. Sometimes the ghost appears as an apparition or as simply a dark shape. On some occasions a voice is heard to utter groans or curses. Fragrances are smelled, and objects are moved. The ghost may appear to a single individual or an entire group. And if the truth be told, with all of the scientific investigation, their non-existence has never been proven.

People accept without question what scientists discover about matter. No one has ever seen an electron or a tachyon, yet evidence points to their existence. Likewise, evidence points to the existence of a spirit world.

It is not a world that haunts the physical but embraces it with vitality.

If these things are true and we are forced to believe in them simply because they are there, it will change our perceptions of the true nature of humanity and its destiny. We will never know until we begin to open the doors and explore those realms.

10

IMPORTANT PRECAUTIONS

There is a responsibility in working with the spirit realm. You can open up to it, but it is not always that easy to close down, especially if you opened to it in an incorrect manner. Keep in mind that psychic and clairvoyant ability does not necessarily include high moral character. There are ignorant mediums and psychics. That is why it is better for you to develop the ability yourself, or at least learn to "try the spirits." A psychic or medium can introduce you to some of your spirit guides, but he or she should not be your sole intermediary.

Use discernment. There are ways of determining whether or not what you are impressed with is mere fancy or is valid. If valid, the information will be verifiable on some level. Confirmation will come to you through other sources or by events working out as told by spirit. Negative spirits will not communicate smoothly. The experience will be unpleasant and uncomfortable. It will create stress. Those spirits which are negative are more likely to approach you during times of dilemma, so greater discrimination is required at such times.

Join a meditation or development group. If you do not feel comfortable with the group after several meetings, keep searching until you find one in which you do feel comfortable. There are many wonderful groups out there. Unfortunately, there are also a few negative, almost cult-like groups as well. You probably will never encounter them, but be aware that they do exist.

Those negative groups always have certain common characteristics and strategies. They recognize that if they can institute a behavior, they can get you to change a belief. Beware of the following:

- A group that wants you to make sudden changes in your environment. This leads to suggestibility and changes in your basic beliefs.
- A group that pushes you into making important decisions without giving you time to think about them.
- A group or individual that requires absolute obedience.

• A group or individual that makes claims of divinity or of special knowledge.

If the group tries to separate or alienate you from friends and family, something is wrong. Beware of sessions that leave you exhausted or drained. If there is a lack of privacy a warning bell should go off.

Always ask questions, no matter how silly or stupid you may think they are. I know it is cliche, but there is no such thing as a stupid question. Focus on your own activities and development and don't open yourself to personal confessions. Always maintain outside contact and work with the everyday world. Remember that you have the right and the need to say "NO!" to anything that makes you feel uncomfortable.

Opening to the spirit realm is not something to dabble with! It is not a parlor game. You can enjoy the development process, but you must learn to respect it. Use the exercises as much as possible for the first few months. Meditate just to maintain balance and relieve stress. Use the Middle Pillar Exercise frequently for balance and energy. Once you begin to open to the spirit realm, do not go to spirit too often or for every decision. Moderation is the key.

There are many people who work to develop their sensitivity so they can do psychic readings. There is nothing wrong with this, but there is a great responsibility. Here are some specific concerns that should be looked at:

1. Make sure you get some formal counseling training. You may get intuitive impressions and messages from spirit, but you must know how to present them so that the individual can use the information. A good 85 per cent of those who would come to you are coming because of real problems and not necessarily for psychic information. The counseling and the psychic work should go hand in hand.

2. Don't work with spirit too often. It is easy to become dependent upon them. You must live your life. They can assist, but you must live it. Be active in your life and in your spirit guide work.

3. Don't provide consultations for others too frequently. They will become dependent upon you rather than living their own lives. I generally will not read or consult for someone more often than once a year. For most

people, there is not enough change to warrant it. I tell them if specific questions or concerns arise, just give me a call, otherwise there is no need to do a full consultation.

4. Don't use your spirit guide contact as a crutch or become superstitious about it. Do not allow those you counsel with to do this either.

5. Do not make decisions for others or tell them what to do. Interpret and mediate, but do not direct! What you say can take on greater importance when there is that psychic connection which occurs during a consultation or reading. Remain detached and avoid, as much as possible, personal preferences, likes and dislikes.

6. *Always* honor client confidentiality! No one but you and the individual have the right to know what goes on in the session. If the other person wishes to tell others fine, but you do not have that right. It is a matter of trust.

7. Let the person know that there is free will. You may, with the help of your spirit guides, be able to pinpoint a pattern or particular flow of energy and the events com-

ing into the individual's life, but it is not engraved in stone.

8. Use a traditional sandwich technique. Start with the positive. If there is a troublesome or negative area, deal with it in the middle. Do it in a manner that reveals options and possible solutions. It should reinforce hope. The end should *always* be more positive!

Discerning False Channeling

There are a number of important considerations in any spirit contact, especially anything which involves trance mediumship or channeling. It may only be the ego of the individual that is manifesting and not an actual entity. The key is not *who* is coming through but *what* information. It may be a personality from a person's previous life possibly indicating a splintering of the present personality which came into this life with the past synthesized. This will lead to further splintering. Many individuals use names that are exotic—appealing to humanity's ability to find spiritual excitement through a guru.

We should ask ourselves some important questions, just to be on the safe side. Remember we are working with a realm that is new and uncharted:

1. Do we have the right to allow other entities to use the vehicle we have taken upon ourselves to grow and develop? If it is a master or high teacher, do they need the body of a human to communicate? Remember that many masters appeared to their followers after death. They were not channeled. If they could do it then, they can do it now.

2. Do you not understand the material but accept it blindly because it sounds educated? If so, something is wrong.

3. Are you expected to accept what is brought through simply because the entity was a high teacher—even though this cannot be proven? It is not unusual for exotic names and times to be used which can't be proven one way or the other.

4. Does the individual provide additional teachings or simply reflections of other teachings? Are teachings provided that have no possibility of verification? A true teacher or master will expect you to test the spirits.

5. Are vague and distant prophecies presented that stimulate uncomfortable emotions? This can be a form of manipulation.

6. Is the material presented ever contradictory to what was presented before by this individual or by other recognized teachers and masters?

7. Is the message engineered beautifully or does it have more of an emotional appeal? Is it always flattering?

8. Does the individual live up to the standards he or she presents in the channelings?

If there has been inappropriate channeling or an awakening to it, certain effects will be discernible. Usually this will reveal itself anywhere within a three to seven year period. A variety of nerve and health problems will begin to manifest. Hypersensitivity, an increase in personal problems and other imbalances will become apparent. (Many will explain and excuse these as part of their initiatory process, but initiation involves learning to maintain balance within the new growth.)

It will become increasingly difficult for the individual to hide imbalances. There will be increasing concern and focus on material and personal gain. The individual will develop a spirit of criticism and begin to distort teachings, even attacking the teachings of others.

An attitude of, "I have my spiritual sources and others are not able to work on the planes that I am" will become increasingly clear.

Discrimination and learning to independently test everything is the key. This requires education in the whole process of spiritual thought and activity. And this requires much time and effort.

Discerning True Soul Impression and Intuition

True spirit contact and soul intuition will always be in the nature of inspiration and relate itself to service. It energizes, stimulates creativity, vitality and a sense of joy. Those who have opened to it properly are identified by certain characteristics:

1. The individual becomes increasingly magnetic, drawing more and more people to him or her. There is no diminishing. Their field of service continually grows.

2. You will understand all that you receive and will be able to agree with it based on your own basic knowledge.

3. There is always a new teaching, angle or approach, and greater depth, synthesis, etc.

4. The individual will demonstrate humility, sincerity and simplicity. He or she lives to the highest standard. He or she does not need to be perfect, but it should be evident that that is a goal. They do not make self-claims nor do they make demands on others.

5. Contact with these individuals will always stimulate strong, positive intuitive and mental responses. They are like power-houses of energy. They encourage, heal and protect others.

6. Those with true spirit contact and soul intuition are highly organized. They have developed minds, hearts and intuitive abilities. They are creative in many avenues and they have many years of service.

7. There will be increasing work with the *law of privacy*. The individual may attune to you and pick up impressions on you, but he or she will not reveal it because of higher law. They recognize their power to influence others and so are extremely cautious about what is expressed. They may see, but they won't tell you what they see. They may not directly reveal things to you, but their energy will so stimulate your own intuition that

you will be able to see and understand more clearly.

A person with good spirit contact and developed soul faculties will not only see impressions of you and your life, but will also see how you will likely respond to that information. Thus it is couched in a manner that the other person can best work with it.

Contact with the spirit realm is always memorable. It strengthens the will and enlightens the mind. It gives greater meaning to life and awakens a new sense of duty. It helps us to remember that the finger pointing at the sun is not the sun!

The purpose of spirit contact is not for psychic power or public demonstrations. Its purpose is to look beyond the physical limitations of life and learn the creative possibilities that exist within them while at the same time transcending them. Its purpose is to help us rediscover the wonder, the awe and the power that is available within our life.

BIBLIOGRAPHY

_____. *Devas and Men*. Theosophical Publishing House, Adyar, 1977.

Basil, Robert, Ed. *Not Necessarily the New Age*. Prometheus Books, Buffalo, 1988.

Bradley, Dorothy and Robert, M.D. *Psychic Phenomena*. Parker Publishing Co., New York, 1969.

Bradley, Marion Zimmer. *The Mists of Avalon* Ballantine, New York, 1982.

Briggs, Katherine. *Encyclopedia of Fairies*. Pantheon Books, New York, 1976.

Davidson, Gustav. *Dictionary of Angels*. The Free Press, New York, 1967.

Dennings, Melita and Phillips, Osbourne. *The Development of Psychic Power*. Llewellyn Publications, St. Paul, 1981.

Evans, W.H. *How to Be a Medium*. Lumen Press, St. Louis, N.D.

Finucane, R. C. *Appearances of the Dead*. Prometheus Books, Buffalo, 1984.

Ford, Arthur. *Unknown but Known.* Harper & Row, New York, 1968.

Garfield, Laeh Maggie & Grant, Jack. *Companions in Spirit.* Celestial Arts. Berkeley, 1984.

Haining, Peter. *Dictionary of Ghost Lore.* Prentice-Hall, Englewood Cliffs, 1984.

Hall, Manly P. *The Blessed Angels.* Philosophical Research Society, Los Angeles, 1980.

Hall, Trevor. *The Medium and the Scientist.* Prometheus Books, Buffalo, 1984.

Hawken, Paul. *Magic of Findhorn.* Bantam Books, New York, 1975.

Hodson, Geoffrey. *Fairies at Work and Play.* Theosophical Society, Wheaton, 1982.

_____. *Brotherhood of Angels.* Theosophical Society, Wheaton, 1982.

_____. *Kingdom of the Gods.* Theosophical Society, Adyar, 1952.

Holzer, Hans. *Ghosts I've Met.* Bobbs-Merrill Co., New York, 1965.

_____. *Life After Death: The Challenge and Evidence.* Bobbs-Merrill Co., Indianapolis, 1969.

Kardec, Allan. *Book of Mediums.* Samuel Weiser, New York, 1970.

Klimo, Jon. *Channeling.* Jeremy Tarcher, Los Angeles, 1987.

Larsen, Stephen. *The Shaman's Doorway*. Harper and Row, New York, 1976.

Larson, Bob. *Straight Answers on the New Age*. Thomas Nelson Pub., Nashville, 1989.

Leadbeater, C.W. *The Invisible Helpers*. Theosophical Publishing, Adyar, 1973.

Maclean, Dorothy. *To Hear the Angels Sing*. Lorian Press, Middleton, 1980.

Newhouse, Flower. *Rediscovering The Angels*. Christward Ministry, Escondido, 1976.

Puryear, Herbert. *The Edgar Cayce Primer*. Bantam Books, New York, 1982.

Roberts, Nancy. *Haunted Houses*. Globe Pequot Press, Chester, 1988.

Roman, Sanaya & Packer, Duane. *Opening to Channel*. H.J. Kramer, Tiburon, 1987.

Ryerson, Kevin & Harolde, Stephanie. *Spirit Communication*. Bantam Books, New York, 1989.

Saraydarian, Torkom. *Psyche and Psychism, Vol. I & II*. Aquarian Education Group, Sedona, 1981.

Sitwell, Sacheverell. *Poltergeists*. Dorset Press, New York, 1959.

Van Gelder, Dora. *The Real World of Fairies*. Theosophical Pub., Wheaton, 1977.

Wolfe, Amber. *In the Shadow of the Shaman*. Llewellyn Publications, St. Paul, 1988.

STAY IN TOUCH

On the following pages you will find listed, with their current prices, some of the books now available on related subjects. Your book dealer stocks most of these and will stock new titles in the Llewellyn series as they become available. We urge your patronage.

To obtain our full catalog, to keep informed about new titles as they are released and to benefit from informative articles and helpful news, you are invited to write for our bimonthly news magazine/catalog, *Llewellyn's New Worlds of Mind and Spirit*. A sample copy is free, and it will continue coming to you at no cost as long as you are an active mail customer. Or you may subscribe for just $7.00 in the U.S.A. and Canada ($20.00 overseas, first class mail). Many bookstores also have *New Worlds* available to their customers. Ask for it.

Stay in touch! In *New Worlds'* pages you will find news and features about new books, tapes and services, announcements of meetings and seminars, articles helpful to our readers, news of authors, products and services, special money-making opportunities, and much more.

Llewellyn's New Worlds of Mind and Spirit
P.O. Box 64383-008, St. Paul, MN 55164-0383, U.S.A.
* * *

TO ORDER BOOKS AND TAPES

If your book dealer does not have the books described on the following pages readily available, you may order them directly from the publisher by sending full price in U.S. funds, plus $3.00 for postage and handling for orders *under* $10.00; $4.00 for orders *over* $10.00. There are no postage and handling charges for orders over $50.00. Postage and handling rates are subject to change. UPS Delivery: We ship UPS whenever possible. Delivery guaranteed. Provide your street address as UPS does not deliver to P.O. Boxes. UPS to Canada requires a $50.00 minimum order. Allow 4-6 weeks for delivery. Orders outside the U.S.A. and Canada: Airmail—add retail price of book; add $5.00 for each non-book item (tapes, etc.); add $1.00 per item for surface mail.

LLEWELLYN PUBLICATIONS
P.O. BOX 64383-008
St. Paul, MN 55164-0383, U.S.A.

HOW TO HEAL WITH COLOR
by Ted Andrews

Now, for perhaps the first time, color therapy is placed within the grasp of the average individual. Anyone can learn to facilitate and accelerate the healing process on all levels with the simple color therapies in *How to Heal with Color*.

This book provides color application guidelines that are beneficial for over 50 physical conditions and a wide variety of emotional and mental conditions. Receive simple and tangible instructions for performing "muscle testing" on yourself and others to find the most beneficial colors. Learn how to apply color therapy through touch, projection, breathing, cloth, water and candles. Learn how to use the little known but powerful color-healing system of the mystical Qabala to balance and open the psychic centers. Plus, discover simple techniques for performing long distance healings on others.

0-87542-005-2, 240 pgs., mass market, illus. $3.95

HOW TO UNCOVER YOUR PAST LIVES
by Ted Andrews

Knowledge of your past lives can be extremely rewarding. It can assist you in opening to new depths within your own psychological makeup. It can provide greater insight into present circumstances with loved ones, career and health. It is also a lot of fun.

To explore your past lives, you need only use one or more of the techniques offered. Complete instructions are provided for a safe and easy regression. Learn to dowse to pinpoint the years and places of your lives with great accuracy, make your own self-hypnosis tape, attune to the incoming child during pregnancy, use the Tarot and the Cabala in past life meditations, keep a past life journal and more.

0-87542-022-2, 240 pgs., mass market, illus. $3.95

HOW TO SEE AND READ THE AURA
by Ted Andrews

Everyone has an aura—the three-dimensional, shape-and-color-changing energy field that surrounds all matter. And anyone can learn to see and experience the aura more effectively. There is nothing magical about the process. It simply involves a little understanding, time, practice and perseverance.

Learning to see the aura not only breaks down old barriers—it also increases sensitivity. As we develop the ability to see and feel the more subtle aspects of life, our intuition unfolds and increases, and the childlike joy and wonder of life returns.

0-87542-013-3, 160 pgs., mass market, illus.   **$3.95**

THE LLEWELLYN PRACTICAL GUIDE TO THE DEVELOPMENT OF PSYCHIC POWERS
by Denning & Phillips

You may not realize it, but you already have the ability to use ESP, astral vision and clairvoyance, divination, dowsing, prophecy, and communication with spirits.

Written by two of the most knowledgeable experts in the world of psychic development, this book is a complete course—teaching you, step-by-step, how to develop these powers that actually have been yours since birth. Using the techniques, you will soon be able to move objects at a distance, see into the future, know the thoughts and feelings of another person, find lost objects and locate water using your no-longer latent talents.

The text shows you how to make the equipment you can use, the exercises you can do—many of them at any time, anywhere—and how to use your abilities to change your life and the lives of those close to you. Many of the exercises are presented in forms that can be adapted as games for pleasure and fun, as well as development.

0-87542-191-1, 272 pgs., 5 1/4 x 8, illus., softcover $8.95

ESP, WITCHES & UFOS:
The Best of Hans Holzer, Book II
Edited by Raymond Buckland
In this exciting anthology, best-selling author and psychic investigator Hans Holzer explores true accounts of the strange and unknown: telepathy, psychic and reincarnation dreams, survival after death, psycho-ecstasy, unorthodox healings, Pagans and Witches, and Ufonauts. Reports included in this volume:

- Mrs. F. dreamed of a group of killers and was particularly frightened by the eyes of their leader. Ten days later, the Sharon Tate murders broke into the headlines. When Mrs. F. saw the photo of Charles Manson, she immediately recognized him as the man from her dream
- How you can use four simple "wish-fulfillment" steps to achieve psycho-ecstasy—turning a negative situation into something positive
- Several true accounts of miraculous healings achieved by unorthodox medical practitioners
- How the author, when late to meet with a friend and unable to find a telephone nearby, sent a telepathic message to his friend via his friend's answering service
- The reasons why more and more people are turning to Witchcraft and Paganism as a way of life
- When UFOs land: physical evidence vs. cultists

These reports and many more will entertain and enlighten all readers intrigued by the mysteries of life ... and beyond!

0-87542-368-X, 304 pgs., mass market   **$4.95**

THE LLEWELLYN PRACTICAL GUIDE TO ASTRAL PROJECTION
by Denning & Phillips

Yes, your consciousness can be sent forth, out-of-the-body, with full awareness and return with full memory. You can travel through time and space, converse with non-physical entities, obtain knowledge by non-material means, and experience higher dimensions.

Is there live-after-death? Are we forever shackled by time and space? The ability to go forth by means of the Astral Body, or Body of Light, gives the personal assurance of consciousness (and life) beyond the limitations of the physical body. No other answer to these ageless questions is as meaningful as experienced reality.

The reader is led through the essential stages for the inner growth and development that will culminate in full conscious projection and return. Not only are the requisite practices set forth in step-by-step procedures, augmented with photographs and puts-you-in-the-picture visualization aids, but the vital reasons for undertaking them are clearly explained. Beyond this, the great benefits from the physical and emotional health, mental discipline, spiritual attainment, and the development of extra faculties. Guidance is also given to the Astral World itself: what to expect, what can be done-including the ecstatic experience of Astral Sex between two people who project together into this higher world where true union is consummated free of barriers of physical bodies.

0-87542-181-4, 272 pgs., 5¼ x 8, illus., softcover $7.95